6.95

Applied Demand Analysis

Longman Economics Series
Series editors: Robert Millward, Michael T. Sumner
and George Zis

Applied Demand Analysis

R. L. Thomas

Longman
London and New York

Longman Group UK Limited
Longman House, Burnt Mill, Harlow
Essex CM20 2JE, England
and Associated Companies throughout the world

Published in the United States of America
by Longman Inc., New York

First published 1987

British Library Cataloguing in Publication Data
Thomas, R. L. (Richard Leighton)
  Applied demand analysis (Longman
  economics series)
  1. Demand (Economic theory)—Econometric
  models
  I. Title
  338.5′212   HB141
  ISBN 0-582-29723-0

Library of Congress Cataloging in Publication Data
Thomas, R. Leighton, 1942–
  Applied demand analysis.
  (Longman economics series)
  Bibliography: p.
  Includes index.
  1. Demand (Economic theory)—Econometric
models.
  2. Consumption (Economics)—Econometric models.
  I. Title.   II. Series.
  HB801.T525 1987   338.5′212   86-10422
  ISBN 0-582-29723-0

Produced by Longman Singapore Publishers (Pte) Ltd.
Printed in Singapore

Contents

Contents

Preface

Econometric demand analysis has been a rapidly expanding area of research during the past quarter-century. However, the relatively mathematical nature of the subject has tended to make it inaccessible to most undergraduates and to many non-specialised postgraduates. This is unfortunate since there are few areas of economics where theory has had such an influence on applied work.

I have endeavoured in this book to provide a text that, while not shirking the mathematics required, will be intelligible to the non-specialist. The level is pitched deliberately below that of the excellent textbook by Deaton and Muellbauer (1980a) and the coverage is not as wide. However, the aim is to provide a comprehensible introductory text rather than an exhaustive coverage of the subject. Deaton and Muellbauer could be regarded as the 'next step' for anyone whose interest is aroused.

Logically, the treatment of single demand equations should perhaps come after the consideration of complete systems. I have reversed the order in this book because pedagogically some topics are more easily approached by this route. I have also attempted a blend of the original 'fundamental matrix equation approach' and the newer cost function approach to systems of demand equations. While the cost function approach is undoubtedly easier, I believe that the original approach still provides some valuable insights.

I am indebted to Mike Pearson and an anonymous referee for comments on earlier drafts of the book and to Shirley Woolley for her immaculate typing. Needless to say, any errors that remain are my own.

R.L.T. December 1985

Acknowledgements

We are indebted to the following for permission to reproduce copyright material:
Cambridge University Press for Tables 1.1 & 1.2 from Table 106 pp. 326–7 *Measurement of Consumer Exp. and Behaviour in UK 1920–38* Vol. 1, 1954, by J. R. N. Jones and Table 1.3 from Table 10 p. 94 *The Analysis of Family Budgets* (1955), by S. J. Praise & H. Houthhakker; Harvard University Press for Table 1.4 from *Consumer Demand in the US 1929–70* 2nd edition 1970, by H. Houthhakker & L. O. Taylor.

Introduction

The estimation of demand equations provides the earliest example of the use of statistical techniques on economic data. The Marshallian analysis of markets in terms of demand and supply curves naturally suggests that attempts should be made to estimate empirically the slopes of such curves and efforts to do so date back as far as Moore (1914). The importance of such empirical work should be relatively obvious. Firms and industries require accurate forecasts of the future level of demand for their output. Governments may find that forecasts of aggregate consumption expenditure may be inadequate since identical levels of such expenditure may have different impacts on the economy, depending on their composition. For example, if some types of consumer expenditure have a greater import content than others then the composition of expenditure will have implications for a country's total import bill.

It is possible to identify two distinct approaches to the estimation of demand equations. The first and original approach concentrates on the demand for a particular commodity or commodity group, paying great attention to any special characteristics of the single market involved. The second approach, developed almost entirely since the 1960s, involves the simultaneous estimation of complete systems containing demand equations for every commodity group purchased by consumers.

Interest in the complete system approach arises for both theoretical and practical reasons. Theoretically the demand for any good depends on the prices of all goods, but data limitations make it impossible to include all such prices in any empirical demand equation. For this reason such equations are generally specified in a relatively *ad hoc* manner with little reference to any underlying theory of consumer behaviour. Normally explanatory variables are restricted to own-price, the prices of a very limited number of close substitutes or complements and an income or total expenditure variable.

The complete system approach has a sounder theoretical base. In a complete system each equation again contains as explanatory variables the prices of all goods. Unrestricted estimation of such systems is therefore just as impractical as the estimation of a single demand equation under similar conditions. However, the theory of consumer behaviour provides a series of restrictions which the equations of a complete system must theoretically satisfy – for example, the sum of the price elasticities and the total expenditure elasticity must be zero for each commodity. The imposition of these restrictions significantly reduces the number of independent price and income responses that have to be estimated. For example, given estimates of the price elasticities for each commodity, expenditure elasticities may be calculated.* Moreover, a

---

* In any but the smallest system, these restrictions alone would still leave too many independent responses for estimation to be possible. However, provided certain assumptions can be made about the structure of consumer preferences, additional restrictions may be derived that further reduce the number of independent responses in the system.

well-known theorem in econometrics implies that the imposition of such restrictions (provided they are valid) improves the efficiency of the estimating procedure and enables more precise estimates of the parameters of each demand equation to be obtained. The crucial point, however, is that the majority of these restrictions are 'cross-equation' restrictions – that is, they involve the parameters of more than one equation. Hence they cannot be imposed if each equation is estimated in isolation. Thus the estimation of a complete system of demand equations in principle enables us to obtain better estimates of each equation in the system than if we approach each single equation in isolation.

We shall begin by considering the 'single equation approach' to demand analysis, partly because of chronological reasons, but mainly because the 'complete system approach' is better appreciated if we proceed by this route.

1 The estimation of single demand equations

The number of econometric studies of individual demand equations is so large that a complete survey is virtually impossible. We therefore restrict ourselves to considering the general problems involved and to indicating some of the techniques that have been used in attempts to overcome these problems. We refer to particular studies only when such studies involve aspects of especial interest.

1.1 Specification of the demand equation

Before attempts are made to estimate a demand equation some consideration must be given to its specification. For example, we have to consider the number and type of explanatory variables to be included and the various functional forms that can be given to the equation. It is natural to turn, hopefully, to economic theory for help in such matters.

The neo-classical static theory of consumer behaviour[1]* tells us that the utility maximising consumer's demand for any commodity is dependent on the price of all commodities available to him and on his total expenditure on these commodities (which, for the moment, we take as given). That is,

$$q_i = \phi_i(p_1, p_2, \ldots p_i, \ldots, p_n, m) \qquad i = 1, 2, \ldots, n \qquad [1.1]$$

where q_i is the quantity demanded of the ith commodity, p_i is its price, $m = \Sigma \, p_i q_i$ is total expenditure and there are n commodities in all. As we have noted, the majority of the restrictions on equations [1.1] which are implied by consumer theory are cross-equation restrictions. So, if we are considering just a single demand equation, theory is not particularly helpful. It does, however, tell us that the demand for any commodity is homogeneous of degree zero in prices and total expenditure – that is, if all prices and total expenditure change proportionately then there should be no change in quantity demanded. Also the Slutsky equation tells us that own-price substitution effects should always be negative.[2] That is, if a consumer is compensated so as to maintain his utility constant, he always responds to a rise in the price of a good by reducing his demand for it. This is the famous 'law of demand' and, in terms of price and income derivatives, implies that

$$\frac{\partial q_i}{\partial p_i} + q_i \frac{\partial q_i}{\partial m} < 0.$$

Thus if a demand equation is to be consistent with theory its derivatives must

---

* Superior figures refer to Notes given at the end of the chapter.

3

generally obey this restriction. Finally, there is the obvious restriction (nevertheless frequently ignored) that expenditure on any one commodity cannot exceed total expenditure. Thus the form of the demand equation should be such that the restriction $p_i q_i < m$ should hold at all points.

Consumer theory unfortunately tells us nothing about the precise functional form of equation [1.1]. This will depend on the consumer's preferences about which little is known *a priori*. Moreover, preferences change over time and so, therefore, will the demand equation. However, provided such changes are gradual, we might hope to account for them by the inclusion of time trends in the demand equation. Another difficulty is that to know theoretically that all prices appear in the demand equation is not very helpful from an empirical point of view. Sample sizes are not unlimited and degrees-of-freedom problems often preclude use of more than a small number of explanatory variables.

The typical response of investigators to the 'unhelpfulness' of underlying theory has been to proceed in an *ad hoc* manner. Firstly, functional forms for the demand equation which most simplify the estimation process are selected, and, secondly, explanatory price variables are limited to own-price, the prices of any close substitutes or complements and/or the general price level. Changes in taste are then allowed for by the inclusion of a time trend as an additional variable. Typical specifications might therefore be:

$$q_i = a_0 + a_1 p_i + a_2 p_j + a_3 p + a_4 m + a_5 t \qquad [1.2]$$

or

$$q_i = A_0 p_i^{a_1} p_j^{a_2} p^{a_3} m^{a_4} e^{a_5 t} \qquad [1.3]$$

where p_j is the price of a substitute or complement, p is an index of the general price level and t is time. Equation [1.2] has the obvious advantage of being linear, while equation [1.3] is linear in the logarithms. Equation [1.3] has the additional advantage that its parameters, the a_i's, represent the quantities which are often of greatest interest in demand studies – the elasticities of quantity demanded with respect to the various explanatory variables.

There is also a difficulty over the interpretation of the variable m which we have so far referred to as total expenditure $\Sigma \, p_i q_i$. Many studies, typically of time series data, employ instead some measure of the consumer's disposable income. If all income were spent, there would be no problem since the two variables would then be identical. However, a considerable proportion of income is not normally devoted to current expenditure but is saved and this leads us to consider the consumer as an intertemporal utility maximiser. If this is the case, current demand for any commodity is theoretically dependent on all current *and* future prices and on some 'total resources' type variable, possibly referring to the whole of the consumer's remaining life-span. Most economists would, nowadays, regard the replacement of such a 'total resources' variable by just current income as a serious mis-specification.[3] However, suppose we can regard the consumer as solving the overall problem of allocating his 'total resources' in two stages – firstly, by deciding on his total *current* expenditure and, secondly, by allocating this already determined total current expenditure between commodities on the basis of their current prices. It is then possible to justify demand equations including, as explanatory variables, just *current* prices and *current* total expenditure. We shall consider later the conditions under which this is theoretically justified.

4

In so far as consumer theory provides restrictions on the form of individual demand equations such as [1.2] and [1.3], the investigator faces the choice of either (a) accepting the restrictions and imposing them prior to estimation, or (b) estimating the equations in their absence and then testing for their validity. In the single equation context, homogeneity is the strongest restriction (in the sense of having the greatest chance of being rejected by the data) and is therefore of the most interest. Imposing homogeneity before estimation implies accepting that demand is a function of *relative* prices and *real* total expenditure and hence replacing equations such as [1.2] and [1.3] by

$$q_i = a_0 + a_1\left(\frac{p_i}{p}\right) + a_2\left(\frac{p_j}{p}\right) + a_4\left(\frac{m}{p}\right) + a_5 t \qquad [1.2A]$$

and

$$q_i = A_0\left(\frac{p_i}{p}\right)^{a_1}\left(\frac{p_j}{p}\right)^{a_2}\left(\frac{m}{p}\right)^{a_4} e^{a_5 t} \qquad [1.3A]$$

Notice that for the logarithmic formulation, imposing homogeneity implies imposing the restriction $a_1 + a_2 + a_3 + a_4 = 0$.

Alternatively, if [1.2] and [1.3] are estimated in unrestricted form, then homogeneity is most easily tested using equation [1.3] since, given homogeneity, the sum of the elasticities in this equation should equal zero. If this sum is significantly different from zero then homogeneity is rejected.

Most single equation studies have in fact concentrated more on estimation than on hypothesis testing, and the most popular procedure has been to work in terms of relative prices and real income. This has the advantage of increasing the available degrees of freedom by one and, by reducing the number of price variables, limits any problems of multicollinearity that may arise. While enforcing homogeneity is common procedure, it is very rarely, however, that any attempt is made to impose the negativity of the own-price substitution effect. This is presumably because of the greater difficulty of imposing an inequality-type restriction as opposed to an equality.

Finally, attention is hardly ever paid to the restriction that the demand equation should be such that $p_i q_i < m$. For example, the logarithmic formulation [1.3] can normally only hold over a restricted range of m. This is because for luxury goods (with a total expenditure elasticity $a_4 > 1$) equation [1.3] implies that there is always some sufficiently high value for m for which $p_i q_i > m$. Similarly, for necessities ($a_4 < 1$) there will always be some sufficiently low value of m which makes $p_i q_i > m$. Indeed, we shall see later that there is normally no way that either the linear formulation [1.2] or the logarithmic formulation [1.3], when used for all commodities in a demand system, can satisfy all the restrictions implied by consumer theory.

1.2 Sources of data and the aggregation problem

As with most estimation problems in economics there are two broad categories of data which can be used in the estimation of demand equations – cross-sectional data and time series data. Cross-sectional data come from the 'budget surveys' carried out regularly in most developed countries. The main aim of these surveys is, nowadays, to determine suitable weights for cost-of-living indices. However, since they involve the collection of information on the pattern of household expenditures, they provide a valuable source of data for the applied econometrician. They are especially useful for concentrating on the manner in which demands vary with household incomes and total expenditures. This is partly because of the wide variation in income levels in a typical cross-section and partly because, since the surveys are carried out within a relatively brief time-span, it is possible to regard all households as facing virtually identical prices for the commodities they purchase. Budget surveys typically cover households from all social classes and all regional areas. They provide exhaustive information on all types of household expenditure, sometimes in minute detail but often in terms of broad commodity groupings, e.g. 'expenditure on food', 'expenditure on clothing', etc.

Prices show very little variation over the budget survey cross-section; therefore, if information is required on the response of demands to changes in prices, it is necessary to resort to time series data. Such data typically describe the responses of large groups of households (often all households in an economy) to variations in incomes and prices over periods of up to twenty or thirty years. Early time series studies tended to concentrate on the demand for staple agricultural products because price and quantity data for such homogeneous commodities were the only data readily available at that time. The estimation of demand equations for heterogeneous manufactured goods such as 'clothing' had to await the general availability of price indices and total expenditure series for these goods. A dependent variable roughly equivalent to 'quantity purchased' could then be constructed for such goods by deflating the expenditure series by the price index.

Time series data generally consist of either annual or quarterly observations and, particularly in the latter case, it may be that such data do not conform to the static nature of traditional consumer theory. An adjustment to a change in prices or income takes time and the period required for adjustment may be larger than one quarter or one year. Time series data are therefore likely to reflect dynamic adjustment processes. Such processes are likely to be particularly important in the case of durable goods but are probably less important for non-durable categories of expenditure such as that on food. For this reason, it will be necessary, later, to devote a separate section to the demand for durable goods.

Consumer theory yields the result that the *individual* consumer's demand for any *individual* commodity can be represented as a function of prices and total expenditure that possesses certain properties. However, almost all available data on prices and quantities purchased are aggregate in nature. Moreover, they are frequently aggregate in two senses. They normally, except in the case of certain basic goods, refer not to individual but to broad groups of commodities. Also, they almost invariably refer to large groups of, rather than individual, households or consumers. This is often as true of cross-sectional data, where budget survey results are usually published for all households within broad income classes, as it is for time series data. Just because theory suggests a relationship between demand, prices and total expenditure at the individual consumer-commodity level, it by no means necessarily follows that an identical or similar relationship will hold for aggregate data. The determination of the conditions under which 'micro-relationships' can be aggregated to form a 'macro-relationship' of the same form is known as the *aggregation problem*.

In the single equation context little attention has been paid to the conditions under which large commodity groupings can be legitimately treated as if they were a single good. The precise conditions under which this is possible are rather restrictive. Fortunately, however, provided commodities are grouped according to the different needs that they satisfy (and most available data satisfy this criterion, e.g. all food items are normally classified under 'food'), it appears that the errors involved in working with such groups rather than with individual goods are not large. We shall return to this problem later, in the context of the complete system approach to demand analysis. The problem of aggregating over individuals, however, requires more immediate attention.

Suppose, for purely expository purposes, that household h's demand for a particular commodity has the following linear form:

$$q^h = a_0^h + a_1^h p + a_2^h p^s + a_3^h m^h \qquad [1.4]$$

where p and p^s are the own-price and the price of a substitute good and m^h is the total expenditure of household h. Other price variables could be included in [1.4] without affecting the following arguments. Also, if necessary, we can regard all price and expenditure explanatory variables as having been deflated by some general price index. Notice, however, that of the explanatory variables only total expenditure has been 'superscripted' by h. We are therefore assuming that while households have different total expenditures, they all face the same prices.

We require the conditions under which, if all households have micro-demand equations like [1.4], there will exist a macro or aggregate relationship of the form

$$\bar{q} = a_0 + a_1 p + a_2 p^s + a_3 \bar{m} \qquad [1.5]$$

where $\bar{q}$ and $\bar{m}$ are the arithmetic means of the households' demands and total expenditures and the a_i's are constants. Notice that in dealing in terms of simple arithmetic means, we are treating all households alike and abstracting, for the moment, from the fact that households in general will differ in both size and composition. If the total number of households is N then we have, from equation [1.4],

$$\bar{q} = \frac{\Sigma q^h}{N} = \frac{\Sigma a_0^h}{N} + \left(\frac{\Sigma a_1^h}{N}\right)p + \left(\frac{\Sigma a_2^h}{N}\right)p^s + \left(\frac{\Sigma a_3^h m^h}{\Sigma m^h}\right)\bar{m} \qquad [1.6]$$

where the summation is over all households and $\bar{m} = \Sigma m^h/N$. Thus, after aggregation we obtain an equation of similar form to the required equation [1.5] where the 'macro-parameters' a_0, a_1 and a_2 are the arithmetic means of the corresponding 'micro-parameters' (i.e. $a_0 = \Sigma a_0^h/N$, etc.) but where a_3 is equal to the quantity $\Sigma a_3^h m^h/\Sigma m^h$. This is a *weighted* mean of the individual micro a_3^h's with weights $m^h/\Sigma m^h$ equal to the proportion of aggregate expenditure made by each individual household. The difficulty is that such a weighted mean depends on the total expenditures of all households and will not normally be a constant. Only if the distribution of total expenditures over time remains constant will the weights $m^h/\Sigma m^h$ be constant, and even then we could not interpret a_3 as being the arithmetic mean of all the a_3^h's unless all households had identical total expenditures.

If we are to have 'perfect' aggregation in the sense that the macro-parameters are not only constants but are all arithmetic means of the corresponding micro-parameters, then it is necessary that $a_3^h = a_3 =$ constant for all households. That is, all households must have the same *marginal propensity to spend* on the commodity in question. When this is the case

$$\frac{\Sigma a_3^h m^h}{\Sigma m^h} = \frac{a_3 \Sigma m^h}{\Sigma m^h} = a_3$$

so that a_3, like the other macro-parameters, is now indeed equal to the mean of corresponding micro-parameters, but we achieve this only because it is equal to each and every such micro-parameter.

The convergence approach to aggregation

The condition for perfect aggregation – equal marginal propensities to spend – is obviously very restrictive and unlikely to be realised in practice. However, if certain less restrictive conditions held it would be possible to obtain a close approximation to perfect aggregation. Suppose the aggregate number of households is *very large* (as is frequently the case) and that the m^h and the a_3^h are *distributed independently across households* (i.e. there is no tendency, for example, for households to have both a large total expenditure m^h and a large marginal propensity to spend a_3^h). Under these conditions, any expenditure weighted mean of the a_3^h's will be very close to the simple arithmetic mean.[4] The larger the number of households, the closer will be the approximation.

The above approach to the aggregation problem is known as the *convergence approach*. The key requirement, however, is the independence of the m^h's and the a_3^h's. If consumers with large total expenditures have high marginal propensities (as tends to be the case with 'luxury' goods), then the expenditure weighted mean will overestimate the arithmetic mean of a_3^h's. Similarly, if total expenditures and marginal propensities are negatively correlated (as tends to be the case with necessities), the expenditure weighted mean will underestimate the arithmetic mean. Unfortunately, since all commodities fall into the categories of luxuries or necessities, the assumption of independence between the m^h's and a_3^h's is, to a lesser or greater extent, likely to break down in practice.

If the m^h's and the a_3^h's are not independent, then this is not too serious provided the relationship between them remains constant over time. The expenditure weighted mean of the a_3^h's would then also remain constant over time, so that the micro-relationship [1.6] will have constant coefficients, although a_3 would not be the arithmetic mean of the a_3^h's. This discrepancy would not matter if we were prepared to accept less than a 'perfect' aggregation in which each macro-parameter bears the same relationship to its corresponding micro-parameters. However, even though a constant relationship over time between the m^h's and the a_3^h's is a little more likely than complete independence, it is clear that the conditions required for even an 'imperfect' aggregation will seldom be realised in practice.

8

Non-linear equations

Aggregation difficulties become even more severe if we abandon linear demand equations such as [1.4]. Suppose, for example, the hth household's demand equation is, instead, merely linear in the logarithms:

$$q^h = A_0(p)^{a_1}(p^s)^{a_2}(m^h)^{a_3} \qquad [1.7]$$

where we have made the simplifying assumption that A_0 and the a_i's are constant for all households. Taking logarithms and summing over all households yields

$$\frac{1}{N} \sum \log q^h = \log A_0 + a_1 \log p + a_2 \log p^s + a_3\left(\frac{1}{N}\right) \sum \log m^h$$

Thus we can only obtain a macro-relationship of similar form to [1.7]; that is

$$\bar{q} = A_0(p)^{a_1}(p^s)^{a_2}(\bar{m})^{a_3}$$

if we define aggregate variables $\bar{q}$ as antilog $(1/N \log q^h)$ and $\bar{m}$ as antilog $(1/N \log m^h)$. This is equivalent to defining the aggregate variables as geometric rather than arithmetic means of the micro-variables.[5] Unfortunately, while it is a simple matter to calculate arithmetic means from aggregate data it is not normally possible to calculate such geometric means, although it is sometimes possible to make use of known relationships between the two. When it is not possible to transform a demand equation into a linear relationship, as can be done with [1.7], aggregation difficulties become even greater. Indeed, it should be intuitively clear that if we are to limit ourselves to defining macro-variables as arithmetic means (and data problems leave little alternative), then the individual micro-demands must be linear functions of total expenditure if aggregation, perfect or imperfect, is to be even feasible.

The formidable difficulties posed by the aggregation problem have frequently led to investigators ignoring it and carrying on regardless. An intuitively appealing argument for doing so has in fact been provided by Hicks (1956). Consumer theory, it is argued, can only be applied, if at all, to the 'representative' consumer.

> To assume that the representative consumer acts like the ideal consumer is a hypothesis worth testing; to assume that an actual person, the Mr Brown or Mr Jones who lives around the corner, does in fact act in such a way does not deserve a moment's consideration.

The representative consumer is a statistical average (who need not in fact exist). Hence, to determine the relationship between his demands and his total expenditures we must calculate the arithmetic averages of individual demands and expenditures and consider the relationship between these. Thus we are led back to the approach adopted by most investigators.

We have limited this subsection to considering the conditions necessary for the existence of macro-relationships of the same functional form as the micro-relationships. Unfortunately it is by no means obvious that the macro-relationship (even when it exists) will satisfy the restrictions implied by consumer theory, even when all the micro-relationships do so. That is the macro-relationship may not be derivable from a 'macro-utility function'. In a single equation context, however, the major restriction of interest is that of homogeneity. As we have pointed out above, the variables in equations such as [1.4] can, if necessary, be regarded as relative prices and real total expenditure. Hence, if the micro-relationships satisfy the homogeneity restriction and can be satisfactorily aggregated, then the macro-relationship obtained must also satisfy this restriction.

1.3 The estimation of single demand equations from time series data

Even if we are prepared to ignore problems such as that of aggregation and the correct specification of demand equations, the estimation of a macro-demand relationship from time series data is not quite the straightforward problem it might first appear. Suppose we wish to estimate a demand equation for some non-durable commodity of the form

$$q_t = a_0 + a_1 p_t + a_2 p_t^s + a_3 m_t + u_t \qquad [1.8]$$

where the t subscripts indicate that we are dealing with time series data, and u_t is a random disturbance reflecting any factors other than own-price p_t, price of substitute p_t^s and total expenditure m_t that might influence aggregate quantity demanded, q_t. Suppose, further, that during the time that we collect data on the relevant market, the variables p_t^s and m_t are, purely by chance, constant. We might then hope to observe and estimate the 'demand curve' of the elementary textbook – that is the relationship between quantity demanded and own-price that exists under the *ceteris paribus* assumption that all other relevant variables remain constant. However, the supply curve for a commodity is also a relationship between quantity and own-price drawn up under the *ceteris paribus* assumption. The question therefore naturally arises: What precisely will we be estimating if we carry out, for example, a simple ordinary least-squares regression of quantity on own-price?

To get to the root of this problem, let us suppose we can represent the 'supply equation' for this commodity by

$$q_t = b_0 + b_1 p_t + b_2 w_t + v_t \qquad [1.9]$$

where w_t is some other variable such as 'wage costs' which influences supply. We conveniently assume that the market always 'clears' so that we can represent both demand for and supply of the commodity by q_t. v_t is a disturbance similar to u_t. If we observe this market under *ceteris paribus* conditions then the demand and supply equations are for observational purposes reduced to

$$q_t = a_0' + a_1 p_t + u_t \qquad [1.8A]$$

and

$$q_t = b_0' + b_1 p_t + v_t \qquad [1.9A]$$

where $a_0' = a_1 + a_2 p_t^s + a_3 m_t = $ constant and $b_0' = b_0 + b_2 w_t = $ constant.

It should be clear that if the disturbances in equations [1.8A] and [1.9A] were always identically zero, then all we could ever observe over time, under the stated conditions, would be a single price–quantity combination. That is, a

1.1 Shifting demand and supply curves

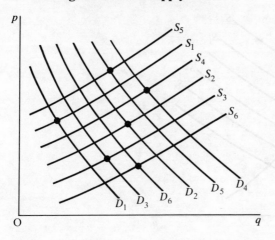

scatter diagram would yield just a single point corresponding to the intersection of fixed demand and supply curves. Even when the two disturbances vary about zero over time, all we can hope to observe is a series of intersection points reflecting continuously shifting demand and supply curves. This situation is illustrated in Fig. 1.1. A line or curve 'fitted' to such a scatter of points will represent neither demand nor supply curve but merely some 'mongrel' curve which is an unspecified combination of both. Note that as far as the two-dimensional Fig. 1.1 is concerned, variations in the disturbances u_t and v_t imply changes in the 'intercepts $a'_0 + u_t$ and $b'_0 + v_t$ of equations [1.8A] and [1.9A]. Hence the shifting curves of Fig. 1.1.

The above is the simplest illustration of what is known as an *identification problem*. Identification of either curve can only be achieved provided it remains stationary over time while the other curve shifts. For example, if the variance of the disturbance v_t in the supply equation happens to be large while that of u_t in the demand equation is very small, this would result in a shifting supply curve 'tracing out' a virtually stationary demand curve as illustrated in Figure 1.2. Alternatively, suppose the *ceteris paribus* assumption were violated to the extent that the 'wage costs' variable in the supply equation fluctuated over time, while the variables p^s and m in the demand equation still remained constant. Then, again, a shifting supply curve would trace out the demand curve.

This 'identification' of the demand curve when w varies over time, may be expressed algebraically as follows. Suppose we multiply equation [1.9] by λ and equation [1.8A] by μ, where λ and μ are *any* two constants. Adding the equations obtained in this way yields

$$q_t = \frac{\lambda b_0 + \mu a'_0}{\lambda + \mu} + \left(\frac{\lambda b_1 + \mu a_1}{\lambda + \mu}\right)p_t + \left(\frac{\lambda b_2}{\lambda + \mu}\right)w_t + \frac{\lambda v_t + \mu u_t}{\lambda + \mu} \qquad [1.10]$$

If equations [1.9] and [1.8A] are acceptable representations of the demand and supply relationships under the given conditions, then equation [1.10] must be equally valid. In addition, equation [1.10] is empirically indistinguishable from the supply equation [1.9], expressing q_t as a linear function of p_t and w_t plus

1.2 Stationary demand curve and shifting supply curve

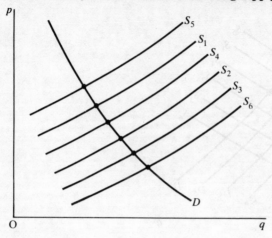

a 'disturbance'. Moreover, since λ and μ can take any values, the model consisting of equations [1.9] and [1.8A] generates an infinite number of such 'mongrel' equations all empirically indistinguishable from the supply equation. Thus if we were to attempt estimation of the supply equation by regressing (by ordinary least-squares or *any other method*) q_t on p_t and w_t, we would have no justification whatsoever for interpreting the coefficients of such a regression equation as estimates of the parameters b_0, b_1 and b_2 in the supply equation. The supply equation is therefore said to be 'unidentified'. Notice, however, that equation [1.10] cannot be confused with demand equation [1.8A], since it includes the variable w_t which does not appear in the demand equation. The demand equation is therefore 'identified' and in principle estimable under the present conditions.

Suppose, however, that conditions had been such that it was the 'wage costs' variable that remained constant over time while the variables p^s and m appearing in the demand equation fluctuated. By a similar procedure we could then derive a mongrel equation like [1.10] which would be indistinguishable from the demand equation but clearly different from the supply equation. That is, the supply equation would now be 'traced out' over time while the demand equation would be unidentified.

It should be clear from the above that an equation (demand or supply) can become identified by the appearance of a variable or variables in the other equation that is or are not present in the first. However, it is necessary for such variables to vary over time if identification is to be achieved in this manner. In practice we are always likely to find variables appearing in the demand equation that do not appear in the supply equation, and vice-versa. However, what matters is the extent to which variables in the model, other than quantity and own-price, vary over time. Identification in practice is a relative rather than an absolute concern. If supply-determining factors tend to vary over time more than demand-determining factors then it is the demand equation that we tend to observe. The greater the variation in the conditions of supply the more

12

sharply is the demand equation identified. Minor variations on the supply side would allow us only a vague and hazy glimpse of the demand relationship.

Fortunately most of the early studies of demand equations were concerned with agricultural commodities for which supply conditions, because of weather factors, crop diseases, etc., are indeed very variable. Hence it is likely that early investigators, even though paying no formal attention to identification problems, were in fact observing demand relationships. However, for manufactured commodities it is by no means certain that supply conditions will show sufficient variation over time to adequately identify a demand relationship. In such cases, therefore, careful consideration needs to be given to the identification problem.

Two points should be made quite clear. Firstly, if an equation is unidentified then, however large the sample size, there is no way in which unbiased estimates of its parameters can be obtained. This applies to all methods of estimation not merely the frequently used ordinary least squares. All so-called 'simultaneous equation estimating methods' are, equally, of no avail in such a situation. We just do not know what we are estimating. Secondly, even if we are satisfied that an equation is identified, then it is normally the case that ordinary least-squares estimators of its parameters will still be biased. This is the problem of *simultaneous equation bias* which needs to be clearly distinguished from the separate but related problem of identification. It is in this situation that the simultaneous equation estimators come into their own since, unlike the ordinary least-squares estimators, they are unbiased provided that the sample size is sufficiently large.

To illustrate this problem of ordinary least-squares bias in the present context, consider the simple two-equation simultaneous system consisting of the identified demand equation [1.8A] and the unidentified supply equation [1.9]. Expressing the model's *endogenous* variables q_t and p_t in terms of the *exogenous* variable w_t we obtain the *reduced form*

$$p_t = \frac{b_0 - a_0'}{a_1 - b_1} + \left(\frac{b_2}{a_1 - b_1}\right)w_t + \frac{v_t - u_t}{a_1 - b_1} \tag{1.11}$$

$$q_t = \frac{a_1 b_0 - a_0' b_1}{a_1 - b_1} + \left(\frac{a_1 b_2}{a_1 - b_1}\right)w_t + \frac{a_1 v_t - b_1 u_t}{a_1 - b_1} \tag{1.12}$$

Notice from equations [1.11] and [1.12] that both the endogenous variables q_t and p_t are dependent on the two disturbances u_t and v_t. In particular, the endogenous variable p_t which appears as an explanatory variable in the demand equation [1.8A] is dependent on the disturbance in that equation. In fact since, normally, we might expect $a_1 < 0$ and $b_1 > 0$, p_t is likely to be positively correlated with u_t. The consequences of this are illustrated in Fig. 1.3.

The broken line represents the underlying demand equation which remains *unknown* but which we wish to estimate. The disturbances u_t represent the vertical deviations from this line of points in a scatter diagram. If values of p_t are positively correlated with values of u_t, then 'high' values of p_t will tend to coincide with 'high' (i.e. positive) value of u_t. Similarly, 'low' values of p_t will tend to coincide with 'low' (i.e. negative) values of u_t. This means we are very likely to observe a scatter of points similar to those represented by the crosses in Fig. 1.3. Remember, all we observe is the scatter of points and not the unknown demand curve. A line fitted to this scatter is therefore likely to

1.3 Biased estimation of the demand curve

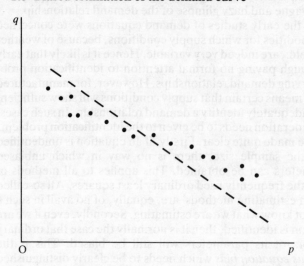

underestimate the downward slope of the demand curve and also to underestimate its intercept and these biases will persist however large the number of points in the scatter. Such bias is generally referred to as 'simultaneous equation bias' and arises because of the simultaneous nature of equations [1.8A] and [1.9].

Simultaneous equation systems almost invariably include endogenous variables on the right-hand side, which are typically correlated with the disturbances of the equations in which they occur (as in Fig. 1.3). Hence, biases of this kind are common in economic models which are frequently of a simultaneous nature.

In most cases, then, even when a demand equation is identified, the application of the ordinary least-squares method of estimation will lead to biased estimates of its parameters. There are, however, two important exceptions to this general rule. The first is the case where supply is 'predetermined'. Consider the market for a perishable agricultural commodity. The supply of such products is virtually perfectly inelastic with respect to current price because of the time required to 'sow and reap' and is also subject to purely exogenous factors such as weather conditions. In such circumstances it is legitimate to replace the supply equation by the statement

$$q_t = q_t^0 = \text{predetermined}$$

Adding a demand equation such as equation [1.8], we now have a model in which the only endogenous variable is own-price p_t. That is, own-price adjusts so as to clear the market for any predetermined q_t^0, p_t^s and m_t. Note that the assumption that the market is always cleared – and hence that we can represent both demand and supply by q_t – is here justified by the fact that the commodity is perishable.

Since q_t^0 is predetermined while p_t is endogenous, an obvious procedure is to rewrite the demand equation with the own-price variable on the left-hand side:

$$p_t = -\frac{a_0}{a_1} + \left(\frac{1}{a_1}\right)q_t^0 - \left(\frac{a_2}{a_1}\right)p_t^s - \left(\frac{a_3}{a_1}\right)m_t - \left(\frac{1}{a_1}\right)u_t \qquad [1.13]$$

All the explanatory variables in equation [1.13] are either predetermined like q_t^0 or are determined exogenously like p_t^s and m_t. They may therefore be assumed to be independent of the disturbance $(1/a_1)u_t$ in equation [1.13], so that ordinary least squares may be applied to this equation without meeting the problem of bias discussed above. Unbiased estimates of the coefficients of [1.13] can therefore be obtained. Estimates of the parameters a_0, a_1, a_2 and a_3 in the original demand equation can then be derived, although these estimates will retain the property of unbiasedness only for large samples.[6] One of the earliest examples of this approach is provided by Fox (1958) who estimated demand elasticities for various food products from US data for 1922–41.

The second case where the simple application of ordinary least squares is appropriate occurs when own-price itself can be regarded as predetermined. This is typically the case when the commodity concerned is a public utility for which price is set by public regulation regardless of cost or supply consider-ations. Since own-price is then no longer endogenous, its presence among the explanatory variables in a demand equation no longer gives rise to bias when the ordinary least-squares method is used. A well-known study carried out under such conditions is that of Fisher and Kaysen (1962) on the US demand for electricity.

It must be stressed, however, that the above are special cases and that the estimation of demand equations normally should involve the use of simul-taneous equation estimating methods. Well-known early studies of simul-taneous demand–supply models which pay special attention to the particular characteristics of the market being studied are Suits' (1955) study of the US water-melon market and the study of the US poultry industry by Fisher (1958).

1.4 Stone's study of pre-war consumers' expenditure in the UK

The classic example of the single-equation approach to demand analysis is probably the massive study by Stone (1954a) of UK consumers' expenditures on non-durables during 1920–38. Whereas single-equation studies generally pay scant attention to theoretical considerations, Stone's work is notable for its attempt to employ theory to refine the estimating equations used. In many ways this study anticipates the later complete system approach. Stone uses a logarithmic demand function similar to equation [1.3] but which, initially (in a theoretically correct manner), includes the prices of all commodities. For commodity i

$$\log q_i = \alpha_i + e_i \log m + \sum_{k=1}^{n} e_{ik} \log p_k \qquad [1.14]$$

where e_i and e_{ik} are total expenditure and price elasticities, respectively, and there are n commodities in all. However, with only nineteen annual time series observations, the number of explanatory variables has to be severely restricted if estimation is to be possible. The standard procedure of excluding all price variables but those of close substitutes or complements is theoretically unacceptable since, although the cross-substitution effects of changes in the prices of unrelated goods may justifiably be assumed to be very small, if all such prices change their income effect is not small. Stone, however, decomposes all the price elasticities into their income and substitution components using the Slutsky equation which in elasticity terms can be written as[7]

$$e_{ik} = e_{ik}^* - e_i w_k \qquad k = 1, 2, 3, \ldots, n \qquad\qquad [1.15]$$

where the e_{ik}^* are the 'compensated' elasticities and $w_k = p_k q_k / m$ is the proportion of total expenditure which goes on the kth commodity. Substituting [1.15] in [1.14] yields

$$\log q_i = \alpha_i + e_i \left(\log m - \sum_{k=1}^n w_k \log p_k \right) + \sum_{k=1}^n e_{ik}^* \log p_k \qquad [1.16]$$

Notice that since $\Sigma\, w_k = 1$, the quantity $\Sigma\, w_k \log p_k$ is a weighted mean of the logarithms of prices. It can be regarded as the logarithm of a general index of prices, p, provided we calculate this general index as a weighted geometric mean of the individual prices. Equation [1.16] can therefore be written as

$$\log q_i = \alpha_i + e_i \log \left(\frac{m}{p} \right) + \sum_{k=1}^n e_{ik}^* \log p_k$$

The only equality-type restriction of interest in a single-equation context is that of homogeneity. Homogeneity implies that the sum of the total expenditure elasticity and all uncompensated price elasticities is zero. Since from [1.15]

$$\sum_k e_{ik}^* = \sum_k e_{ik} + e_i \sum_k w_k = \sum_k e_{ik} + e_i$$

homogeneity also implies that the sum of the compensated price elasticities is zero. Equation [1.16], given homogeneity, can therefore be further rewritten as

$$\log q_i = \alpha_i + e_i \log \left(\frac{m}{p} \right) + \sum_{k=1}^n e_{ik}^* \log \left(\frac{p_k}{p} \right) \qquad [1.17]$$

Since it is quite reasonable to treat the compensated cross-price elasticities of unrelated goods as negligible once we have allowed for income effects, it is now possible to suppress many of the price variables in [1.17] and rewrite it as

$$\log q_i = \alpha_i + e_i \log \left(\frac{m}{p} \right) + e_{ii}^* \log \left(\frac{p_i}{p} \right) + e_{ir}^* \log \left(\frac{p_r}{p} \right) + e_{is}^* \log \left(\frac{p_s}{p} \right)$$

$$[1.18]$$

where goods r and s are close substitutes or complements (their number need not necessarily be restricted to two) and m/p is an index of real income.

Equation [1.18] is Stone's basic equation for the demand for non-durable goods and this is estimated using aggregate UK data for the period 1920–38. No attempt is made to tackle the problem of simultaneous equation bias and ordinary least-squares methods of estimation are used throughout.

Another important feature of Stone's analysis is that, partly to conserve degrees of freedom and partly to reduce the multicollinearity problems arising from having both prices and total expenditure as explanatory variables, use is made of an 'extraneous estimate', $\hat{e}_i$, of the total expenditure elasticity. This is

16

1.1 Income and compensated price elasticities for tea and coffee

Commodity	Income	Tea price	Coffee price	Beer price	Time trend coefficient	R^2
Tea	0.04	−0.26	0.14	0.08	0.003	0.56
	(0.04)	(0.07)	(0.03)	(0.05)	(0.003)	
Coffee	1.42	−0.54	−0.55		−0.010	0.15
	(0.30)	(0.39)	(0.42)		(0.018)	

Source: **Stone, J. R. N.** (1954a), *Measurement of Consumer Expansion and Behaviour in the UK, 1920–38, Vol. 1.* Cambridge University Press.

obtained from cross-sectional budget survey data for the late 1930s, and is used to construct a dependent variable, $\log q_i - \hat{e}_i \log(m/p)$, which is then regressed on the price variables. Stone in fact uses an income variable in place of total expenditure in his time series regressions so that $\hat{e}_i$ has to be rather arbitrarily adjusted downwards to account for this. A time trend is also introduced to account for changes in taste so that [1.18] eventually becomes

$$\log q_i - \hat{e}_i \log\left(\frac{m}{p}\right) = \alpha_i + e_{ii}^* \log\left(\frac{p_i}{p}\right) + e_{ir}^* \log\left(\frac{p_r}{p}\right)$$
$$+ e_{is}^* \log\left(\frac{p_s}{p}\right) + \theta_i t + u_t \qquad [1.19]$$

where t is time and u is a disturbance. Equation [1.19] is in fact first differenced before estimation in an attempt to reduce the consequences of any serial correlation in the disturbances. Stone estimates demand equations for non-durable commodities, in particular for forty-eight different types of food expenditure. Some typical results are shown in Tables 1.1 and 1.2, which give income and compensated price elasticities. Figures in parentheses are estimated standard errors.

The results shown are broadly in line with what one might expect for the pre-war UK. For example, tea is clearly a 'necessity' whereas coffee, with an income elasticity in excess of unity, appears to be a 'luxury'. While oranges and

1.2 Income and compensated price elasticities for oranges and bananas

Commodity	Income	Orange price	Banana price	Dried fruit price	Time trend coefficient	R^2
Oranges	0.92	−0.93	0.36	0.77	0.049	0.61
	(0.17)	(0.25)	(0.28)	(0.31)	(0.025)	
Bananas	0.95	−0.41	−0.62		0.004	0.48
	(0.18)	(0.19)	(0.22)		(0.019)	

Source: **Stone, J. R. N.** (1954a), *Measurement of Consumer Expansion and Behaviour in the UK, 1920–38, Vol. 1.* Cambridge University Press.

bananas both have income elasticities just below unity, such values are high relative to most foods considered. The compensated own-price elasticities are negative in all four cases, thus confirming the 'law of demand'. Closer examination, however, reveals inconsistencies when 'cross equation' comparisons are made. The equation for tea has a positive cross-price elasticity for coffee suggesting that these goods are substitutes, whereas the negative tea-price elasticity in the coffee equation suggests they are complements. A similar problem arises with the orange and banana equations. However, Stone was not, here, concerned with the cross-equation implications of consumer theory, although he was well aware that a system of logarithmic equations was incapable of exactly satisfying all the classical restrictions. Nevertheless, he does test the single-equation homogeneity restriction by re-estimating his equations in unrestricted form and summing the compensated price elasticities. In only two cases were these sums significantly different from zero.

Multi-collinearity and the use of extraneous estimates

The procedure, adopted by Stone, of obtaining extraneous estimates of total expenditure elasticities from cross-sectional data and then using them in a time series study aimed at estimating price elasticities, is one which has frequently been employed. It is often impossible to obtain precise estimates of both total expenditure and price elasticities from time series data alone because of the high multi-collinearity typically found between total expenditure and price variables. Certainly for post-war data both tend to be 'trend' variables rising steadily over time. In addition, if homogeneity is imposed, making the explanatory variables *real* total expenditure and *relative* prices, then there is frequently much greater variation over time in the real expenditure variable than in the relative price variable. When a variable changes little over time it is, not surprisingly, difficult to assess the effect of changes in that variable. As a result, estimates of demand equations using time series data alone typically yield reasonably precise estimates of total expenditure elasticities but estimates of price elasticities which are subject to very large standard errors.

Provided an *unbiased* 'extraneous' estimator of the total expenditure elasticity can be found, this problem can be circumvented. The obvious source of such estimators is cross-sectional data since, for such data, it is a reasonable assumption to regard all consumers as facing identical prices. The procedure is most easily outlined if we consider a simple two-variable demand equation.

$$\log q_i = \alpha_i + e_i \log \left(\frac{m}{p} \right) + e_{ii} \log \left(\frac{p_i}{p} \right) \tag{1.20}$$

Given an extraneous estimate $\hat{e}_i$ of the total expenditure elasticity, the variable $\log q_i - \hat{e}_i \log (m/p)$ may be formed and time series data used to regress this new variable on $\log (p_i/p)$ to obtain an estimate of e_{ii}, the own-price elasticity. Provided the extraneous estimator $\hat{e}_i$ is unbiased, the time series estimator of e_{ii} will also be unbiased. Furthermore, the sampling variance of the estimator of e_{ii} obtained in this way will normally be lower than that of the estimator obtained by the straightforward time series regression of $\log q_i$ on $\log (m/p)$ and $\log (p_i/p)$. As first noted by Durbin (1953), the size of this reduction in sampling variance depends

18

(a) on the extent to which the variance of $\hat{e}_i$ is exceeded by the variance of the estimator of e_i obtained by the straightforward application of ordinary least squares to [1.20], and

(b) on the size of the correlation between log (m/p) and log (p_i/p) in the time series data.

The time series collinearity between the explanatory variables in [1.20] is, as we have seen, typically high. Also the variation in total expenditure over a typical cross-section of households is normally large, so that such data provide fairly precise estimates of e_i (i.e. extraneous estimators with relatively low sampling variances). It follows that, provided unbiased estimators of total expenditure elasticities can be obtained from cross-sectional data, the use of such estimators in conjunction with time series data should result in much greater precision in the estimators of price elasticities. However, obtaining such estimators is not a simple matter and it is to this problem that we now turn.

1.5 The estimation of total expenditure elasticities from cross-sectional data

The study of cross-sectional data obtained from budget surveys dates back to E. Engel (1857) who formulated his famous 'law' that the income elasticity of food is always less than unity. Cross-sectional relationships between expenditure on any commodity and the level of income or total expenditure are therefore normally referred to as 'Engel curves'. Provided the budget surveys are completed during a brief time-span, prices faced by all households can, apart from minor variations due to social and regional factors, be regarded as constant. This enables attention to be focused on the responses of household demand to variations in income or total expenditures. Cross-sectional data, in fact, seldom provide accurate information on household incomes, since responses to questions concerning income are notoriously unreliable. For this reason the explanatory variable in cross-sectional demand studies is almost invariably total expenditure rather than income. However, there are, as we have seen, sound theoretical as well as practical reasons why this is a preferable procedure.

The major difficulty in estimating total expenditure elasticities from cross-sectional data is the existence of a number of 'nuisance' variables which, while they can be regarded as approximately constant over time, are certainly not constant over a cross-section of households. Possibly the most important of these are the size and the composition of households. Other such variables include age, social class, neighbourhood, etc.

If these variables were distributed independently of total expenditure across households, their effects could simply be included in the disturbance term of the estimating equation without affecting the unbiasedness of, for example, ordinary least-square estimators. However, household size is obviously likely to be positively correlated with total expenditure, so that its omission from a demand equation will lead to an upward bias in the ordinary least-squares estimators of total expenditure elasticities. Estimated elasticities reflect variations not only in total expenditure but also those in household size. Correlation between any such nuisance variable and total expenditure will lead to similar

1.4 Sigmoid shaped Engel curve

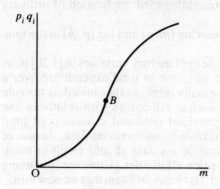

biases. To obtain unbiased estimators it is therefore necessary either explicitly to introduce the relevant nuisance variables into the estimating equation or to concentrate on subsamples of the overall cross-section within which these nuisance variables can be regarded as constant.

We shall return to this problem in a moment, but first let us concentrate on the likely shape of the relationship between expenditure on any single commodity and total expenditure. Many commodities tend to be luxuries at low levels of income and total expenditure but to become necessities as total expenditure increases. Thus we might expect total expenditure elasticities to decline as total expenditure m rises, possibly exceeding unity at low levels of m and maybe even declining to zero at sufficiently high levels of m if a 'saturation' level is reached. A typical Engel curve might be expected to look like that in Fig. 1.4, i.e. it is 'sigmoid' in shape with a point of inflection at B.

In practice, however, a very large variation in total expenditure levels would be necessary to reveal the full sigmoid shape of an Engel curve. For this reason more simple, typically two-parameter, curves are commonly used to approximate whatever portion of the full curve is in fact revealed. The most popular of such curves are the double-logarithmic and semi-logarithmic Engel curves:

$$p_i q_i = A_i m^{\beta_i} \qquad [1.21]$$

$$p_i q_i = \alpha_i + \beta_i \log m \qquad [1.22]$$

The shapes of these functions are illustrated in Fig. 1.5. The double-log function [1.21] has a constant elasticity $e_i = \beta_i$. Curve A illustrates this for $\beta_i > 1$ and curve B for $0 < \beta_i < 1$. These are often suitable approximations for the lower parts of the sigmoid curve before the elasticity shows a pronounced tendency to decline. The semi-log function [1.22] has an elasticity $e_i = \beta_i/(p_i q_i)$ which (assuming a non-inferior good) therefore *declines* as total expenditure rises. Such a curve intersects the m-axis at the point where $\log m = -\alpha_i/\beta_i$ and hence can represent commodities which are not purchased until total expenditure reaches some threshold level. An example of such a function is given by curve C in Fig. 1.5.

Although many other functional forms have been used for the estimation of Engel curves, [1.21] and [1.22] have proved the most successful. For example Prais and Houthakker (1955), in an early classic study of UK cross-sectional

1.5 Logarithmic and semi-logarithmic Engel curves

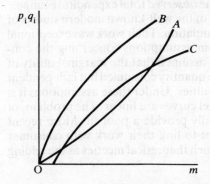

data, experimented with five functional forms but eventually rejected all but the double-log and semi-log forms. In fact they found that for food items, which tend to become necessities at relatively low levels of total expenditure, the semi-log curve provided better fits than the double-log curve. However, for non-food items the double-log form proved more satisfactory.

The income elasticities obtained for six broad food aggregates using the semi-log and double-log forms are shown in Table 1.3.[8]

Notice that the elasticity estimates are broadly similar for both types of function. This reflects the fact that the choice of non-linear function generally seems to have little effect on the size of estimates of total expenditure elasticities.

Engel curves typically have expenditure rather than quantity purchased as the dependent variable. However, since the price of the commodity concerned, p_i, can be regarded as the same for all households, we may convert equations [1.21] and [1.22] above, for example, into 'demand equations' of the same functional form by dividing throughout by p_i.

A more serious problem with both semi-log and double-log functions is that they fail to satisfy the 'adding up' restrictions. That is, if all Engel curves are of either of these forms then the sums of expenditures on all commodities would not equal total expenditure, i.e. $\Sigma p_i q_i \neq m$. In fact, the only form of Engel curve for which the ordinary least-squares method of estimation will yield estimates which automatically satisfy this requirement are *linear* in total expenditure *m*. However, when non-linear functions are fitted to *data* which

1.3 Cross-sectional income elasticities

Food Type	Farinaceous	Dairy	Vegetables	Fruit	Fish	Meat
Semi-log	0.35	0.48	0.58	1.03	0.76	0.62
Double-log	0.36	0.53	0.62	1.20	0.84	0.69

Source: **Praise, S. J. and Houthakker, H.** (1955) *The Analysis of Family Budgets*, Cambridge University Press.

satisfy the condition $\Sigma\ p_i q_i = m$, the resultant estimated *functions* will approximately satisfy this condition over the *observed* total expenditure range.

Allen and Bowley (1935), in the earliest of the well-known modern studies of Engel curves, did in fact adopt a linear formulation. Their work was exceptional in that their Engel curve was derived from assumptions concerning the consumer's utility function. Specifically, they assumed that the marginal utility of each commodity was linearly related to the quantity consumed but independent of the quantity consumed of other commodities. Under these assumptions it is not difficult to show that the resultant Engel curves are linear. The problem, of course, is that linear Engel curves generally provide a poor fit. More recent investigators have abandoned any attempt to link their work with consumer theory in favour of superior fits, ignoring such theoretical niceties as the adding up criterion.

Equivalent adult scales

We turn now to the problems of household size and composition, the nuisance variables to which most attention has been given in the estimation of Engel curves. Other such variables have normally either been dealt with by concentrating on subsamples within a full cross-section or by the simple use of dummy variables – for example, Stone in the work discussed above used a dummy variable to account for differences between professional and working classes.

One obvious method of dealing with the household size problem is simply to include a household size variable, H, in the estimating equation. This, however, raises the question of how we are to measure H. Obviously we cannot simply count the number of individuals in a household. For consumption purposes we cannot regard a household consisting of, for example, two adults and two children as twice the size of one containing just two adults. In the early days of Engel curve estimation much use was made of so-called 'equivalent adult scales'. That is, the size of a household was defined as $H = \Sigma_j \lambda_j n_j$ where n_j is the number of individuals of the jth kind and λ_j is the 'weight' attached to the jth type of individual. Conventionally λ_j for an adult male was set equal to unity and the weights for other individuals were calculated according to nutritional requirements. For example, Stone, in the above study, used the so-called 'Amsterdam Scale' to calculate H for his cross-sectional work. This scale assigned weights of 0.9 to an adult woman and weights, rising with age, from 0.14 to 0.90 for children below the age of 14. The problem with such scales is not just that they are inappropriate for non-food commodities but that they also have a 'normative' aspect. Just because nutritional experts believe that an adult female is equivalent to 0.9 of an adult male, it does not follow that actual households will implicitly adopt such a scale when they allocate a proportion of expenditure to food.

A further problem that arises when a family size variable is included as a separate variable in estimating equations is that of multi-collinearity. A high correlation between household total expenditure and size is to be expected, and this is likely to reduce severely the precision of estimates of total expenditure elasticities. An alternative is to work in terms of expenditures 'per equivalent adult household'. For example, in the case of the semi-log form the Engel curve becomes

$$\frac{p_i q_i}{H_i} = \alpha_i + \beta_i \log\left(\frac{m}{H}\right) \qquad [1.23]$$

where $H_i = \Sigma_j \lambda_{ij} n_j$ is household size calculated using an equivalent adult scale *appropriate to the ith commodity* and $H = \Sigma_j \lambda_j n_j$ is a general scale used to deflate the total expenditure variable. The equivalent adult weights, λ_{ij}, are known as the *specific weights* for the ith commodity and the λ_j as *general* weights.

The λ_{ij} and the λ_j, however, are not determined prior to the estimation process as with the nutritional type scale just described. Notice that equation [1.23] implies that a doubling of both total expenditure and 'general' household size has no effects on demand per equivalent adult household. This means that 'economies of scale' in terms of household size have been ruled out and hence the various scales on which size is determined must be constructed so as to make this assumption a valid one. To do this the scales must necessarily be estimated from the data rather than externally determined, otherwise equations such as [1.23] are most unlikely to represent the data adequately.

One possible procedure is an iterative one which makes use of the fact that, as Prais and Houthakker (1955) have shown, the general weights are weighted averages of the specific weights with weights approximately equal to the budget shares $p_i q_i/m$ of the various commodities. As an illustrative example suppose there are only two types of household, one consisting of an adult male and the other of an adult male plus an adult female. Assigning general and specific weights of unity to an adult male (i.e. $\lambda_1 = 1$ and $\lambda_{i1} = 1$ for all i) we wish to determine the weights λ_2 and the λ_{i2} for an adult female. The semi-log Engel curve [1.23] is then for commodity i

$$\frac{p_i q_i}{1 + \lambda_{i2} n_2} = \alpha_i + \beta_i \log \frac{m}{1 + \lambda_2 n_2} \qquad [1.23A]$$

where n_2 is the number of adult females in the household (n_1, the number of adult males, is unity, by assumption, for all households). Hence,

$$\frac{p_i q_i}{\alpha_i + \beta_i \log m/(1 + \lambda_2 n_2)} - 1 = \lambda_{i2} n_2 \qquad [1.24]$$

Suppose preliminary estimates of β_i are available for each commodity (obtained maybe by estimating [1.23A] under the assumption $\lambda_2 = \lambda_{i2} = 1$) and for the general weight for an adult female ($\lambda_2 = 1$ will do). The quantity on the left-hand side of equation [1.24] can then be computed for each commodity and for every household. For each commodity, this quantity can then be regressed (with intercept suppressed) on n_2 (which is, in effect, a dummy variable taking the value unity when a household contains an adult female and zero otherwise). In this way preliminary estimates of λ_{i2} for each commodity can be obtained. Since general weights are weighted averages of specific weights, the estimates of the λ_{i2} can then be used to obtain a second estimate of λ_2. Equation [1.23A] can now be re-estimated for each commodity to obtain 'second-round' estimates of the β_i's. The process is then repeated until all estimates converge on to stable values.

23

Unfortunately, as first noted by Forsyth (1960), if the form of the Engel curves is such that they satisfy the adding-up restriction then the iterative procedure breaks down because the specific weights become unidentified.[9] For n goods we have to estimate n specific weights from n Engel curves. However, if prices do not vary over the cross-section and if the adding-up criterion is to be satisfied, the Engel curves provide only $n - 1$ independent pieces of information. The ratios of the specific weights are therefore identified but not their absolute sizes.

More recently, Pollack and Wales (1981) have made a thorough examination of methods by which demographic variables such as family size and age composition can be incorporated into demand systems. They examine five possible procedures for introducing the variable 'number of children' using British household budget data for 1966–72. They come down in favour of a version of the Prais–Houthakker technique described above, but where the specific weights were the same for all goods and hence equal to the general weights.

1.6 Interpretational difficulties in the use of extraneous estimators

Even if it is believed that unbiased estimates of total expenditure elasticities have been obtained from cross-sectional data there are certain problems of interpretation that have to be considered before such estimates can be inserted in a time series equation. Firstly, the question arises of whether the total expenditure elasticity obtained from a cross-section of households of varying total expenditure at *a given point in time* is conceptually similar to that which would be exhibited by a single household or group of households as total expenditure varies *over time*. It is often argued that cross-sectional elasticities are 'long run' elasticities whereas those derived from time series data are essentially 'short run'.

Consider two households in a cross-section, the first with a considerably larger total expenditure than the second. Suppose now that the financial circumstances of the second household are transformed overnight so that it began to make the same total expenditure as the first. In the short run, before this household was able to adjust to its new circumstances, habit or inertia might leave the composition of its expenditure little changed. It is only in the long run that its expenditure pattern might become similar to that of the first household. Since it is a reasonable assumption that the majority of households in a cross-section are fairly well adjusted to their financial circumstances, it is likely that cross-sectional data will yield estimates of long-run elasticities. However, when household expenditures increase over time, the influence of habit and inertia can no longer be dismissed so that it may well be that time series elasticity estimates are of a predominantly short-run nature.

The above argument does not mean it is impossible to employ cross-sectional estimates validly in a time series equation. However, such estimates need to be used with great caution, ideally, with allowance being made for the influence of habit and inertia when dealing with time series data, so as to make the two elasticity concepts comparable. We shall return to this problem in the next section.

A further difficulty concerns variations in the quality of commodities. Engel curves are generally estimated for relatively heterogeneous commodities with household expenditure rather than quantity purchased as the dependent variable. For example, expenditure on 'meat' may involve the purchase of a low-quality 'cut' or a high-quality 'cut'. Suppose rises in the total expenditure of a household are accompanied by a switching from lower to higher quality varieties of a commodity. Then increases in expenditure will exceed increases in the 'quantity' purchased, since the higher quality varieties tend to be more highly priced. Prais and Houthakker, in the study already referred to, in fact used, as an index of the quality of a household's purchases of a commodity, a weighted sum of the prices of the different varieties of the commodity. The weights used were proportional to the quantities purchased by the household of each variety. Using this measure of quality, it is not difficult to show that the elasticity of expenditure $[\partial(q_i p_i)/\partial m] \cdot (m/q_i p_i)$ on any commodity is equal to the sum of the elasticities of quality and quantity purchased. A normal Engel curve yields the elasticity of expenditure rather than that of quantity purchased. However, the latter elasticity can also be estimated provided the normal expenditure type dependent variable is deflated by the quality index.

Difficulties arise because the prices and quantities purchased of different varieties of a commodity are often not known. It is then not possible to calculate a quality index. Hence we frequently have to make do with cross-sectional elasticities of expenditure rather than quantity. However, when dealing with time series data, the dependent variable generally has to be defined as 'real expenditure'. That is, expenditure is deflated by a price index to allow for the variation of prices over time and hence to better approximate the 'quantity purchased' of theory. Since any price index will tend to move in the same direction over time as the unknown quality index, time series estimation tends to provide elasticities of quantity purchased rather than expenditure. The effect of quality changes is largely eliminated by the deflation process. Thus, ideally, it is an extraneous estimate of quantity purchased that is required for insertion into a time series equation. Unfortunately such estimates are frequently unobtainable.

Finally there are two more obvious problems. Cross-sectional data often covers only certain social classes within the total population. The question therefore arises of whether elasticities estimated from such data should be inserted into a time series equation to be estimated from aggregate data covering the whole population. Lastly, as we pointed out earlier, cross-sectional data typically provide estimates of total expenditure elasticities, whereas most time series investigators, rightly or wrongly, tend to include income rather than total expenditure in their estimating equations. The procedure normally adopted to get round this discrepancy is to multiply the cross-sectional estimate of the total expenditure elasticity by some independently derived estimate of the elasticity (assumed constant) of total expenditure with respect to income. This yields the required extraneous estimate of the income elasticity. For example, Stone, in the study described above, multiplied all total expenditure elasticities by the constant fraction 0.9 before using them in this time series work.

1.7   Dynamic adjustments and the demand for durable goods

The traditional neo-classical theory of consumer behaviour is static in nature, yielding equilibrium values for quantities demanded and implying an instantaneous adjustment to new equilibrium values in response to price or total expenditure changes. In practice, however, consumers frequently adjust only gradually to such changes, i.e. there are 'lags' involved in their movement to a new equilibrium. There are two main reasons for such lags – the durability of many consumer goods and the existence of habits developed as a result of past consumption.

The fact that stocks of durable goods last for more than one 'period' means that past purchases influence present behaviour and that present behaviour has implications for the future. For example, if a household has just purchased a new washing machine and the following week the price of such goods declines, static theory suggests the household will increase expenditure on washing machines. However, in practice the household is likely to delay the purchase of another new washing machine and maintain expenditure on such items below its new 'equilibrium level' for some considerable time.

The above example well illustrates many of the difficulties involved in the theoretical treatment of durable goods. Unlike most non-durable goods, demands for which can reasonably be treated as continuous variables, the typical consumer durable is very much a discrete quantity. A household cannot increase expenditure on such items by purchasing one-twentieth of a washing machine. It should be clear that a distinction has to be made between *purchases* of a durable good and the *consumption* of the *services* that it yields. It is the consumption of these services that yields utility. Purchases add to the *stock* of the durable good in the possession of consumers while the consumption of services yielded (frequently assumed to be proportional to the size of the stock) leads to a depreciation, i.e. a physical deterioration or depletion, in the stock. Since the stock is depleted over time, a useful distinction has to be made between purchases which represent a *replacement* demand corresponding to the depletion in the stock and purchases which represent a new demand which leads to a net increase in the stock.

If rental markets for all durable goods existed, so that consumers merely hired the flow of services provided by durables, then neo-classical theory could be applied with little difficulty. The rental prices of services could be used to play the same role as the prices of non-durable goods. However, consumers typically purchase consumer durables rather than merely renting them. Nevertheless it is possible to adopt neo-classical theory, albeit at the cost of some strong assumptions, to the analysis of durable goods. Diewert (1974) for example, employs the concept of 'user cost' as a measure of the price paid for the services of a durable good that has in fact been purchased by the consumer.

User cost is calculated as follows. Suppose the durable good depreciates at a constant rate of δ per period. Thus one unit of the good at the beginning of period t becomes equivalent to $1 - \delta$ units of the good at the beginning of period $t + 1$. Suppose v_t and v_{t+1} are the purchase prices of the good at the beginning of periods t and $t + 1$. The user cost p_t of the services obtained from owning one unit of the good during period t is then the difference between the purchase price at the beginning of the period and the discounted price at which the depreciated good could be sold at the beginning of period $t + 1$:

$$p_t = v_t - \frac{(1 - \delta)v_{t+1}}{1 + r} \qquad [1.25]$$

where r is the rate of interest at which it is assumed that the consumer can borrow and lend without limit.[10]

Thus, if the consumer's utility function is defined over the quantities purchased of non-durables and the services consumed of durables, then neo-classical theory can still be applied with p_t as defined in [1.25] playing the role of the price of services yielded by durables. Notice, however, that if equation [1.25] is to be an adequate representation of this rental price then some powerful assumptions are necessary. The type of depreciation assumed precludes any 'vintage effects'. That is, units of the durable good purchased at the beginning of period $t + 1$ are assumed to be of identical quality (i.e. provide the same services per period) as those purchased at the beginning of period t. Thus S washing machines of age equal to one period are exactly equivalent to $(1 - \delta)S$ brand-new washing machines. Furthermore, the consumer is assumed to be able to buy and sell durable goods at the same price. That is, he is able to sell a one-year-old washing machine for $1 - \delta$ times the price at which he can purchase a new one. A perfect market for second-hand durables is therefore implicit in the model.

Even if these assumptions are swallowed the model still has some strange properties. It is possible for user costs, unlike the prices of non-durables, to become negative. This will occur when v_t is sufficiently lower than v_{t+1} for the prospect of capital gains to outweigh interest charges and depreciation. The utility maximising consumer would then wish to consume an infinite quantity of the services provided by the good (i.e. hold an infinite stock of the good). Although the assumption of given and fixed v_t could hardly hold up in the face of such infinite demand, the model does suggest that very large fluctuations in demands for durable goods are likely. That such fluctuations do not occur in practice suggests that instantaneous adjustments to new equilibrium values in response to changes in user cost do not in fact take place. This could be the result of inertia on the part of consumers, imperfect information, or the existence of important costs of adjustment when rapidly moving to new equilibria.

Partial adjustment models

The idea that adjustment to new equilibrium values is non-instantaneous and that only a partial adjustment occurs during any given period of time is the basis of the so-called stock-adjustment models. These models were among the first to be used in the empirical study of the demand for durables and date back to the work of Chow (1957) and (1960), Stone and Rowe (1957) and Nerlove (1958). Chow, for example, in a study of the US demand for automobiles, begins with the assumption that the equilibrium or desired per capita stock of automobiles, S_t^*, is a linear function of per capita real disposable income, y_t, and the relative price of automobiles, p_t:

27

$$S_t^* = \alpha_0 + \alpha_1 p_t + \alpha_2 y_t \qquad\qquad [1.26]$$

However, the actual stock, S_t, is not normally equal to the desired stock. Changes in the actual stock per period are assumed to be only some fraction, λ, of the difference between desired stock and the actual stock of the previous period. Actual stock is only partially adjusted to its equilibrium level during the period:

$$S_t - S_{t-1} = \lambda[S_t^* - S_{t-1}] \qquad 0 < \lambda < 1 \qquad\qquad [1.27]$$

The extent of the adjustment depends on λ. If $\lambda = 1$, then $S_t = S_t^*$ so that adjustment is complete. At the other extreme, if $\lambda = 0$, $S_t = S_{t-1}$ so that no adjustment takes place, however large the difference between desired and actual stock. In general, the larger is λ the greater is the adjustment.

The stock is assumed to depreciate at a constant rate δ per period, so that stocks are related to purchases of new automobiles per capita, q_t, in the following manner:

$$S_t = (1 - \delta)S_{t-1} + q_t \qquad\qquad [1.28]$$

Equation [1.28] can be rewritten so as to express purchases as the sum of net additions to stock and depreciation or 'replacement' purchases.[11]

$$q_t = S_t - S_{t-1} + \delta S_{t-1} \qquad\qquad [1.29]$$

From [1.26], [1.27] and [1.29] an equation for q_t can be derived which does not involve the unobservable desired stock S_t^* and hence, in principle, can be estimated:

$$q_t = \lambda[S_t^* - S_{t-1}] + \delta S_{t-1}$$
$$= \lambda\alpha_0 + \lambda\alpha_1 p_t + \lambda\alpha_2 y_t + (\delta - \lambda)S_{t-1} \qquad\qquad [1.30]$$

Thus, purchases of new automobiles depend not only on price and income but also on the stock of old automobiles carried over from the previous year. Chow constructed a series for the stock variable by taking a weighted sum of total registrations with weights proportional to the prices of used cars of different ages, thus dealing with the 'vintage' problem of having automobiles of varying ages in the total stock. Given an estimate of the depreciation factor δ, obtained by comparing the prices of cars of different ages, he was then able to estimate all the parameters in equation [1.30].

Frequently, however, adequate data, with or without allowing for vintage effects, on the stock of a consumer durable are unavailable. The procedure first followed by Stone and Rowe (1957), in a study of the demand for UK consumer durables, was to construct alternative series for S_t. Starting with an arbitrary fixed level of stock and using equation [1.28] together with data on purchases, such series can be constructed for various assumed values for δ. The arbitrary starting value of S_t can be absorbed into the intercept in equation [1.30] and the value of δ selected which yields the closest fitting estimated version of equation [1.30].

Alternatively, it is possible to transform equation [1.30] so as to eliminate the stock variable altogether. Lagging [1.30] by one period and multiplying throughout by $1 - \delta$

$$(1 - \delta)q_{t-1} = (1 - \delta)\lambda\alpha_0 + (1 - \delta)\lambda\alpha_1 p_{t-1} + (1 - \delta)\lambda\alpha_2 y_{t-1}$$
$$+ (1 - \delta)(\delta - \lambda)S_{t-2} \qquad\qquad [1.31]$$

Taking [1.31] from [1.30] gives

$$q_t - (1 - \delta)q_{t-1} = \delta\lambda\alpha_0 + \lambda\alpha_1 p_t - (1 - \delta)\lambda\alpha_1 p_{t-1} + \lambda\alpha_2 y_t$$
$$- (1 - \delta)\lambda\alpha_2 y_{t-1} + (\delta - \lambda)\{S_{t-1} - (1 - \delta)S_{t-2}\}$$

However, since $S_{t-1} - (1 - \delta)S_{t-2} = q_{t-1}$ from equation [1.28], we eventually obtain

$$q_t = \delta\lambda\alpha_0 + \lambda\alpha_1 p_t - (1 - \delta)\lambda\alpha_1 p_{t-1} + \lambda\alpha_2 y_t + (1 - \delta)\lambda\alpha_2 y_{t-1}$$
$$+ (1 - \lambda)q_{t-1} \tag{1.32}$$

an equation which expresses current purchases as a function of current and lagged income and price variables and lagged purchases. There are problems, however, in the estimation of equation [1.32]. Firstly, it is over-identified. By this we mean that the ratio of the estimated coefficients on the price variables is likely to yield a different estimate of δ from that obtained from the ratio of the estimated coefficients on the income variables. Secondly, if a non-autocorrelated disturbance term is added to equation [1.26] then the transformation to equation [1.32] will result in an autocorrelated disturbance in that equation. This, combined with the presence of the lagged dependent variable, q_{t-1}, on the right-hand side of [1.32], means that least-squares estimates of this equation will be biased even for large samples.

The state-adjustment model

Notwithstanding the estimation difficulties, equation [1.32] has been extensively used in the analysis of durable goods. The stock-adjustment model is an attractive, although *ad hoc* (in the sense that it is not derived from any utility maximising behaviour) method of explaining the importance of lagged variables in estimated demand equations. However, there are other dynamic models which give rise to equations such as [1.32] and in practice it may be difficult to discriminate between them. For example, Houthakker and Taylor (1970) suggest that an equation of the form

$$q_t = \gamma_0 + \gamma_1 p_t + \gamma_2 y_t + \beta S_{t-1} \tag{1.33}$$

can be regarded as holding for all goods both durable and non-durable. S_t is referred to as a *state* variable with a different interpretation for durable and non-durable goods. For durables, S_{t-1} is the beginning period stock of the relevant good so that in this case [1.33] can be regarded as arising out of a stock-adjustment process and is identical to equation [1.30] with $\beta = \delta - \lambda$. For non-durables, however, S_{t-1} is to be interpreted as a 'psychological stock of habits' implying that tastes and hence purchases are influenced by previous consumption. The parameter β is positive for a non-durable habit-forming good. Stocks of habits are determined by

$$S_t = (1 - \delta)S_{t-1} + q_t \qquad 0 < \delta < 1 \tag{1.34}$$

which is identical to equation [1.28] except that δ is now to be interpreted as the rate of decay of habits. This is assumed to occur at a constant proportional rate. Further purchases add to the stock of habits.[12] Successive substitution in [1.34] for S_{t-1}, S_{t-2}, etc., in fact yields

$$S_t = q_t + (1 - \delta)q_{t-1} + (1 - \delta)^2 q_{t-2} + (1 - \delta)^3 q_{t-3} + \cdots$$

Thus the current stock of habits is seen to depend on current and past purchases but, since $1 - \delta < 1$, the further in the past that the purchases were made the less they contribute to the current stock of habits.

Combining equations [1.33] and [1.34] in the same manner as [1.29] and [1.30] yields

$$q_t = \delta\gamma_0 + \gamma_1 p_t - (1 - \delta)\gamma_1 p_{t-1} + \gamma_2 y_t - (1 - \delta)\gamma_2 y_{t-1}$$
$$+ (1 + \beta - \delta)q_{t-1} \qquad [1.35]$$

This is an identical estimating equation to [1.32] except that the coefficients are to be interpreted differently in the case of habit-forming goods.

Houthakker and Taylor regard durable goods which are non-habit-forming as having $\beta < 0$. Notice that this is slightly different to a normal definition since, for example, in the Stone–Rowe model durables would have $\beta > 0$ if $\delta > \lambda$.[13] The advantage of the present model is that equation [1.35] can be applied to any good whether it is durable, habit-forming or, more usefully, *both*. In the last case the sign of β depends on the net effect of the two properties. For example, a negative β implies that 'inventory effects' outweigh 'habit-forming effects'. However, this flexibility makes it possible to rationalise many estimated values for the underlying parameters which might initially seem unlikely. For example, in the stock-adjustment model, a value of λ which exceeds unity or an unreasonably high value for δ, the depreciation rate on durables, can both be explained away by referring to habit-forming effects. Nevertheless, at least the magnitude and, more importantly, the sign of estimates of β has an unambiguous interpretation since this determines the relationship between long- and short-run elasticities. The long-run demand relationship can be derived by setting $S_t = S_{t-1}$ in [1.28] or [1.34], in which case $q_t = \delta S_{t-1}$ (purchases are just sufficient to offset depletions) and then substituting for S_{t-1} in [1.33]. Rearranging yields

$$q_t = \frac{\delta\gamma_0}{\delta - \beta} + \left(\frac{\delta\gamma_1}{\delta - \beta}\right)p_t + \left(\frac{\delta\gamma_2}{\delta - \beta}\right)y_t \qquad [1.36]$$

The long-run effect of changes in income or prices is, therefore, $\delta/(\delta - \beta)$ times the short-run effect. Thus, a negative β means that short-run elasticities are greater than long-run elasticities while a positive β (assuming that $\beta < \delta$, as found in all such cases by Houthakker and Taylor) implies that long-run elasticities are greater. The marked differences found between short- and long-run elasticities were regarded by Houthakker and Taylor as an important justification for their use of a dynamic model.

Houthakker and Taylor estimated equations for 81 categories of consumer expenditure using annual per capita US data in constant prices for the period 1929–64, omitting the war years 1942–45. Their version of the above model is originally formulated in continuous terms (this has the advantage of avoiding problems over goods which depreciate completely within one year) but a discrete approximation is derived for estimating purposes. For 65 of the 81 goods the state-adjustment model provided the best fitting equation. Total expenditure (used as the y_t variable) was found to be a significant determinant of demand in 79 of the 81 cases. Price effects, however, were found to be less important, price variables being significant in only 44 cases.

Of the 65 cases analysed by the state-adjustment model, 46 goods proved to have positive β coefficients and hence larger long-run than short-run elas-

1.4 Long-run and short-run income and price elasticities

	Income elasticities		Price elasticities	
	Short run	Long run	Short run	Long run
Automobiles and parts	5.06	1.07		
Clothing and shoes	1.20	0.35		
Transportation	0.41	0.47	−0.82	−0.95
Food and beverages	0.72	0.85		
Household operations	0.62	5.53	−0.39	−3.44

Source: **Houthakker, H. and Taylor, L. D.** (1970) *Consumer Demand in the US 1929–70*, 2nd edition, Harvard University Press.

ticities. These goods represented 61 per cent of total consumers' expenditure in the US in 1964, suggesting that in aggregate habit-forming effects were more important than net inventory effects. Houthakker and Taylor also estimate their model for a much broader classification of total expenditure, using this time just eleven wider categories. Some examples of the short- and long-run elasticities obtained are shown in Table 1.4.

Notice, that, as might be expected, the durable goods in the top half of the table have smaller long-run than short-run elasticities. This reflects the negative β coefficients found for these goods. The reason for these smaller long-run responses is that, while initially purchases may increase sharply in response to rises in income or falls in price, such increases have important effects on the stocks of durables held. This leads to lower levels of purchases in the future. The categories in the lower half of the table appear to be commodities where habit effects outweigh any inventory effects. The mechanism here is that initial purchases increase the psychological stock of habits. This has the effect of reinforcing future demand so that in this case long-run effects are the larger.

Limitations of the adjustment models

Although the adjustment models described above represent a definite advance on the static neo-classical model, they omit to allow for several factors important in the analysis of the demand for durables. For example, the models have nothing to say concerning the importance of expectations about the future price of durable goods. The prospect of capital gains or losses was emphasised by the generalisation of the neo-classical model described at the beginning of this chapter. The expectation of future changes in durable good prices may well influence the level of demand even if only to the extent that it influences the timing of replacement purchases. The stock-adjustment model virtually defines replacement demand as a given proportion of the beginning period stock. However, replacements may be postponed or advanced as economic conditions warrant and the more recent 'discretionary replacement' models first presented by Smith (1975) and Westin (1975) view replacement in this way.

One obvious omission in the discussion so far concerns the effect of government credit restrictions and other borrowing constraints. In stock-adjustment models such factors are usually handled by adding further variables to equation [1.26] as additional determinants of the optimal capital stock. However, financial factors may well make their influence felt via the speed at which adjustment takes place. The adjustment parameter λ is usually assumed to be constant, but in reality must surely depend on economic variables. Indeed, little attention is paid to the precise reasons for non-instantaneous adjustment – whether, for example, it is the result of information or search costs or due to supply or borrowing constraints.

Many of these problems of formulation arise out of the *ad hoc* nature of the stock-adjustment models and there would appear to be two possible ways forward. Firstly, non-instantaneous adjustment could be regarded as arising out of the utility maximising procedure – to be a natural process to the rational consumer. This would involve redefining the utility function – in the case of habit-forming goods to include past consumption levels. Alternatively, where partial adjustment is the result of supply constraints or financial and liquidity restrictions, rather than introduce these factors via the utility function, it may be more appropriate simply to add further constraints to the normal budget constraint, forming additional restrictions on the utility maximising process.

Notes

1. The neo-classical theory is described in some detail at the beginning of Chapter 2.
2. See pages 45 and 48.
3. The distinction between the two is, of course, the basis of the permanent income and life-cycle hypotheses of the aggregate consumption function.
4. We can write the relevant term in [1.6] as

$$\left(\frac{\Sigma \, a_3^h m^h}{\Sigma \, m^h}\right)\bar{m} = \frac{\Sigma \, a_3^h m^h}{N}$$

If a_3^h and m^h are independently distributed then $E a_3^h m^h = E a_3^h E m^h$. Thus for large N

$$\frac{\Sigma \, a_3^h m^h}{N} \approx \left(\frac{\Sigma \, a_3^h}{N}\right)\left(\frac{\Sigma \, m^h}{N}\right) = \left(\frac{\Sigma \, a_3^h}{N}\right)\bar{m}$$

Thus the coefficient of $\bar{m}$ in equation [1.6] is approximately equal to $\Sigma \, a_3^h / N$.
5. For example

$$\frac{1}{N} \Sigma \log q^h = \frac{1}{N} (\log q^1 + \log q^2 + \cdots + \log q^N)$$
$$= \log (q^1 q^2 \ldots q^N)^{1/N}.$$

Thus $\bar{q} = (q^1 q^2 \ldots q^N)^{1/N}$, the geometric mean of the individual household demands.
6. For example, if $(1/a_1)$ is an unbiased estimator of $1/a_1$ it does not follow that its reciprocal is an unbiased estimator of a_1.
7. The Slutsky equation in this context divides a total cross price effect into a compensated cross-price effect and an income effect. That is,

$$\frac{\partial q_i}{\partial p_k} = \left(\frac{\partial q_i}{\partial p_k}\right)_{U=\text{constant}} - q_k\left(\frac{\partial q_i}{\partial m}\right) \quad \text{(see equation [2.24])}$$

Multiplying through by p_k/q_i yields [1.15].

8. Since the semi-log function has an elasticity of $\beta_i/(p_i/q_i)$ which varies with the level of expenditure, the elasticities have been calculated at the point of mean expenditure.

9. See also Muellbauer (1974) and (1980).

10. User cost thus combines elements of capital gain or loss, interest charges and depreciation. For example, if $r = \delta = 0$ then $p_t = v_t - v_{t+1}$, the capital loss on the good. If $\delta = 0$ and $v_t = v_{t+1}$ then $p_t = rv_t/(1+r) \simeq rv_t$ the interest foregone by having funds tied up in the good. Finally, if $r = 0$ and $v_t = v_{t+1}$ then $p_t = \delta v_t$, the depreciation cost of holding the good for one period. The concept is, in fact, identical to that used by Jorgenson (1963) in his neo-classical theory of investment.

11. δ can also be regarded as the proportion of the beginning year stock which is scrapped during the year. A replacement purchase in this aggregate context need not necessarily imply that a *given* individual has replaced his old car by a new one. The first δS_{t-1} of total purchases are regarded as replacements for cars scrapped who ever does the purchasing. Total purchases may be less than δS_{t-1} of course, in which case net additions to stock are negative.

12. It might appear that a more general version of [1.34] is $S_t = (1-\delta)S_{t-1} + \theta q_t$. However, the units in which the stock of habits are 'measured' can always be chosen so as to make $\theta = 1$.

13. The difference would in fact disappear if q_t was redefined as *net* purchases (i.e. net of depletions).

2 The estimation of complete systems of demand equations

As noted at the outset, in recent years there has developed a second approach to the estimation of demand equations. This involves the estimation of complete systems of equations covering all current expenditures made by the consumer. This enables use to be made of the various restrictions (single-equation and cross-equation) that the theory of consumer behaviour implies for the parameters of such systems. We begin this chapter by formally outlining the theory of consumer behaviour. Next, we derive a set of *general* restrictions on a system of demand equations which arise simply because the consumer is assumed to maximise utility subject to a budget constraint. Later we discuss further restrictions which can arise when particular assumptions are made about a consumer's preference ordering.

2.1 The theory of consumer behaviour

For simplicity we consider, initially, a two-commodity world in which the consumer maximises a utility function:

$$U = U(q_1, q_2) \qquad [2.1]$$

subject to a budget constraint

$$p_1 q_1 + p_2 q_2 = m \qquad [2.2]$$

where q_1 and q_2 are the quantities consumed of the two goods, p_1 and p_2 are their prices and m is the consumer's total expenditure. p_1, p_2 and m are taken as given in the maximisation process.

To be correct, since utility is an ordinal rather than a cardinal concept and 'utility functions' are defined only up to a monotonic transformation, we should refer not to a 'utility function' but to the 'class of utility functions which are representative of the consumer's ordinal preference ordering' and write equation [2.1] as $f\{U(q_1, q_2)\}$. However, for reasons of style we shall continue to refer to the consumer's 'utility function' and, to avoid needless algebraic complications, continue to use equation [2.1]. When we refer to a particular utility function, which is but one possible representation of an ordinal preference ordering, and wish to refer to properties that are not invariant under all monotonic transformations we shall specifically refer to a '(cardinal) utility function'.

The maximisation of [2.1] subject to [2.2] leads to consumer demand equations for each of the two goods:

$$\left. \begin{array}{l} q_1 = q_1(p_1, p_2, m) \\ q_2 = q_2(p_1, p_2, m) \end{array} \right\} \qquad [2.3]$$

34

The traditional neo-classical approach to deriving equations [2.3] involves the use of the Lagrangian multiplier technique. To obtain the first-order conditions for a maximum we form the Lagrangian

$$\phi = U - \lambda(p_1 q_1 + p_2 q_2 - m)$$

where λ is a Lagrangian multiplier, and differentiate with respect to q_1 and q_2. This yields the so-called optimality conditions[1]†

$$U_1 = \lambda p_1 \quad \text{and} \quad U_2 = \lambda p_2 \qquad [2.4]$$

which, together with the budget constraint [2.2], can be solved to provide equilibrium equations for q_1, q_2 and λ in terms of the given p_1, p_2 and m. The first two of these equations are in fact [2.3] and we write the third as

$$\lambda = \lambda(p_1, p_2, m) \qquad [2.5]$$

The two equations represented by [2.3] represent a 'mini-system' of demand equations, demand in each case being expressed as a function of 'all prices' and total expenditure. The Lagrangian multiplier λ is frequently interpreted as the 'marginal utility of total expenditure', or the increase in 'maximum utility' obtainable per unit increase in m. This may be seen intuitively if we divide the optimality conditions [2.4] by p_1 and p_2 respectively. They may then be written as

$$\frac{\partial U}{\partial(p_1 q_1)} = \frac{\partial U}{\partial(p_2 q_2)} = \lambda$$

which suggests that the additional spending of one unit of m on either good raises utility by λ. Remember, however, that marginal utility, like utility itself, is a cardinal concept and the value of λ obtained out of the maximising process will not be invariant under non-linear transformations of equation [2.1]. Equation [2.5] indicates that λ, like q_1 and q_2, is dependent on p_1, p_2 and m.

As an illustration of the above Lagrangian multiplier technique, suppose the consumer's preference ordering can be represented by the utility function

$$U = q_1^2 q_2^3$$

The optimality conditions [2.4] then become

$$2q_1 q_2^3 = \lambda p_1 \quad \text{and} \quad 3q_1^2 q_2^2 = \lambda p_2$$

Dividing one of these optimality conditions by the other eliminates λ and yields $2q_2 p_2 = 3p_1 q_1$. Substituting in the budget constraint [2.2] then gives the demand equations [2.3] as

$$q_1 = \frac{2m}{5p_1} \quad \text{and} \quad q_2 = \frac{3m}{5p_2}$$

Notice that these demand equations are not as general as they might be since there are no 'cross-price effects'; that is q_1 is independent of p_2 and q_2 is independent of p_1. This is the result of the specific form we have chosen for our utility function. We shall discuss this type of utility function in some detail later.

---

† Superior figures refer to Notes given at the end of the chapter.

2.1 Equilibrium with strictly convex preferences

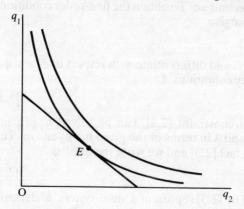

An expression for λ, the marginal utility of total expenditure, can be derived by substituting for q_1 and q_2 in either of the optimality conditions. This yields

$$\lambda = \frac{108m^4}{625p_1^2 p_2^3}$$

Remember, however, that λ is a cardinal concept.

It must be stressed that the validity of the above procedure is crucially dependent on the utility function possessing certain properties. Specifically the utility function [2.1] must be 'strictly quasi-concave'. This implies that the consumer's preference ordering is 'strictly convex' or that the more familiar indifference curves used to represent preferences are *convex to the origin and do not intersect the horizontal or vertical axes*.[2,3] Such preferences are illustrated in Fig. 2.1. The assumption of strictly convex preferences is necessary if it is to be possible to characterise the consumer's equilibrium by a point of tangency between indifference curve and budget line. If this is not possible then the differential calculus approach, which yields an equilibrium at E in Fig. 2.1, will not be applicable.

Figures 2.2 and 2.3 illustrate indifference maps representing preferences

2.2 and 2.3 Possible equilibria with non-strictly convex preferences

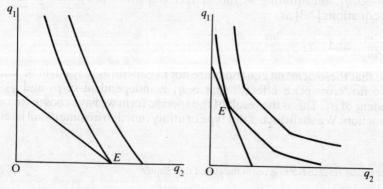

which are not strictly convex. In Fig. 2.2 preferences are convex, but not strictly convex, and the indifference curves, although convex, intersect the horizontal axis. The indifference curves should in fact be regarded as continuing rightwards along the q_2 axis. For the budget line drawn, the consumer's optimal point is clearly at E, which is not a point of tangency. Such a point could not be found using differential calculus. Notice that in such a situation consumption of the first good, q_1, is zero. Only when the price of the first good falls sufficiently for the slope of the budget line to exceed (in absolute terms) that of the indifference curve at E, will some of the first good be purchased. This is, indeed, a perfectly reasonable situation – it is unlikely that a consumer would purchase some of each good no matter what their relative prices.

In Fig. 2.3 the indifference curves are convex to the origin apart from certain linear segments. Along these segments the two goods are simply perfect substitutes for one another. For the budget line drawn, the consumer's optimal point is at the 'kink', E, on the indifference curve, which, again is not a point of tangency.[4] Moreover, if the budget line had happened to be parallel to and coincide with a linear segment, then the consumer's demands would be indeterminate. An infinite number of possible combinations of the two goods would all result in 'maximum utility'. Again neither of these solutions could be found using differential calculus.

It should be clear from the above that, if we are to use the traditional Lagrangian multiplier method to solve the consumer's maximisation problem, *then we require the assumption of strictly convex preferences*. This implies that to obtain a specific functional form for the demand equations [2.3] we have to specify a utility function [2.1] which is strictly quasi-concave. As Figs 2.2 and 2.3 indicate, such assumptions place rather strong and somewhat implausible restrictions on the types of consumer preferences which we can allow for in our analysis. We shall see shortly that an alternative approach is possible that does not require the assumption of convex preferences.

Duality

Much recent work in the analysis of consumer demand makes use of the concept of *duality*. So far, we have expressed the consumer's problem as that of choosing quantities, q_1 and q_2, so as to maximise utility subject to the budget constraint that total expenditure should not exceed a given level m. However, it may be reformulated as that of choosing quantities so as to minimise the total expenditure necessary to achieve a given utility level U.[5] These two problems are frequently referred to as *dual problems* for the following reason. If the former is solved for given m it leads to a set of quantities demanded and a maximum utility level U^*. Also, if the given utility level in the latter problem is set equal to U^*, the solution of this latter problem leads, firstly, *to the same set of quantities demanded* as does the solution to the former problem and, secondly, to a minimum total expenditure level m^* *equal to the given m in the former problem*. In the two-good case the consumer minimises

$$m = p_1 q_1 + p_2 q_2 \qquad [2.6]$$

subject to attaining a given utility level U^*, where

$$U^* = U(q_1, q_2) \qquad [2.7]$$

This yields cost-minimising values of q_1 and q_2 which depend on the prices p_1 and p_2 and on U^*:

$$q_1 = f_1(p_1, p_2, U^*)$$
$$q_2 = f_2(p_1, p_2, U^*)$$

[2.8]

The cost-minimising demand functions [2.8] are normally referred to as *Hicksian compensated demand functions*. They inform us of how price changes affect demand when consumer total expenditure is always simultaneously adjusted so as to keep the consumer at the given utility level, U^*. In contrast, the demand equations [2.3] are known as uncompensated or *Marshallian demand functions*.

Both the solution [2.3] to the utility maximising problem and the solution [2.8] to the cost-minimisation problem can be substituted back into their respective problems. Substitution of equations [2.3] into [2.1] yields the so-called *indirect utility function*

$$U^* = U^*\{q_1(p_1, p_2, m), q_2(p_1, p_2, m)\}$$

[2.9]

Equation [2.9] gives the maximum utility obtainable for any given combination of p_1, p_2 and m. In the general n-good case indirect utility is a function of all n prices and total expenditure. An important property of the indirect utility function is that, since all its arguments (i.e. all the demands q_i) are homogeneous of degree zero in all prices and total expenditure, it is itself homogeneous of degree zero in these variables. To distinguish it from the indirect utility function, the original utility function [2.1] is often referred to as the *direct utility function*.

In a similar manner, equations [2.8] can be substituted back into [2.6] to yield the consumer's *cost function*

$$m^* = p_1 f_1(p_1, p_2, U^*) + p_2 f_2(p_1, p_2, U^*)$$
$$= m^*(p_1, p_2, U^*)$$

[2.10]

Equation [2.10] yields the minimum cost of obtaining the utility level U^* at given prices p_1 and p_2.[6]

As an illustration of indirect utility and cost functions, let us consider again the direct utility function $U = q_1^2 q_2^3$. As we saw on page 35, the Marshallian demand functions corresponding to this direct utility function were $q_1 = 2m/5p_1$ and $q_2 = 3m/5p_2$. Substituting for q_1 and q_2 in $U = q_1^2 q_2^3$ hence yields the indirect utility function [2.9] as

$$U^* = \left(\frac{2}{5}\right)^2 \left(\frac{3}{5}\right)^3 \frac{m^5}{p_1^2 p_2^3}$$

[2.9A]

Notice that U^* is homogeneous of degree zero in p_1, p_2 and m.

To derive the cost function we must treat the consumer as a cost minimiser. Total expenditure, m, is minimised subject to the constraint that utility obtained is the fixed quantity U^*. That is, we minimise $m = p_1 q_1 + p_2 q_2$ subject to

$$U^* = q_1^2 q_2^3$$

[2.7A]

We now form the Lagrangian

$$H = p_1 q_1 + p_2 q_2 - \mu(q_1^2 q_2^3 - U^*)$$

Setting the derivatives $\partial H/\partial q_1$ and $\partial H/\partial q_2$ to zero and eliminating the Lagrangian multiplier, μ, yields the optimal relationship $2p_2q_2 = 3p_1q_1$. Notice that this is identical to the optimal relationship obtained for the utility maximising problem on page 35. This relationship and the constraint [2.7A] can now be solved for the Hicksian compensated demand equations [2.8]. In this case we obtain

$$q_1 = \left(\frac{2}{3}\right)^{3/5} \left(\frac{p_2}{p_1}\right)^{3/5} (U^*)^{1/5} \quad \text{and} \quad q_2 = \left(\frac{2}{3}\right)^{-2/5} \left(\frac{p_1}{p_2}\right)^{2/5} (U^*)^{1/5}$$

[2.8A]

The consumer's cost function is obtained by substituting the Hicksian demands into the expression for total expenditure. This gives

$$m^* = \left(\frac{2}{3}\right)^{3/5} (U^*)^{1/5} p_2^{3/5} p_1^{2/5} + \left(\frac{2}{3}\right)^{-2/5} (U^*)^{1/5} p_2^{3/5} p_1^{2/5}$$

or

$$m^* = \left[\left(\frac{2}{3}\right)^{3/5} + \left(\frac{2}{3}\right)^{-2/5}\right] (U^*)^{1/5} p_2^{3/5} p_1^{2/5}$$

[2.10A]

Notice that the cost function is very closely linked to the indirect utility function [2.9A]. The indirect utility function can be rearranged to give m in terms of p_1, p_2 and U^*:

$$m = \left(\frac{5}{2}\right)^{2/5} \left(\frac{5}{3}\right)^{3/5} (U^*)^{1/5} p_2^{3/5} p_1^{2/5}$$

Since $(\frac{5}{2})^{2/5}(\frac{5}{3})^{3/5} = (\frac{2}{3})^{3/5} + (\frac{2}{3})^{-2/5}$ this equation is identical to the cost function just obtained. In fact the two functions are always related in this way since they are simply different ways of expressing the same information. *The cost function can always be inverted to yield the indirect utility function and vice versa.*

2.2 Properties of the cost function

The cost function plays a central role in so much recent work on consumer demand that we pay particular attention to its properties.

Firstly, the cost function is homogeneous of degree unity in prices. A doubling of p_1 and p_2, for example, will double the total expenditure necessary to attain a given utility level. Secondly, provided we assume non-satiation, as U^* increases so does the minimum cost of attaining that U^* at given prices. That is, if marginal utilities are positive, then utility can only be increased by consuming more and this requires increased expenditure.

Thirdly, and most importantly, for given U^*, the cost function [2.10] is a concave and increasing function of p_1 for given p_2 and a concave and increasing function of p_2 for given p_1. This property is illustrated in Fig. 2.4 which shows the effect on minimum cost of increases in p_1 when p_2 is held constant. To understand why the cost function takes a concave form, suppose that in response to a rise in p_1 from p_1' to p_1'', the consumer makes no change in q_1 and

2.4 Concavity of the cost function

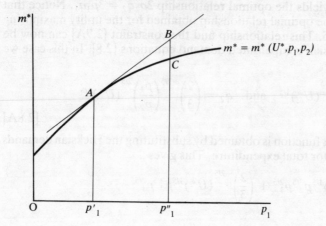

q_2, i.e. remains at the same point on the indifference curve corresponding to the given U^*. The cost of obtaining U^* would then be a linear function of p_1:

$$m = \bar{p}_2\bar{q}_2 + p_1\bar{q}_1$$

where $\bar{q}_2, \bar{q}_1$ and $\bar{p}_2$ are the fixed values of q_2, q_1 and p_2. This linear relationship is represented in Fig. 2.4 by the line tangential to the cost function at A. However, when p_1 rises from p_1' to p_1'', the cost-minimising consumer does not in fact keep q_1 and q_2 unchanged. As implied by equation [2.10], purchases are varied to take advantage of the change in relative prices and hence the rise in cost is *less than linear*. Instead of rising from A to B, the minimum cost of attaining U^* rises from A to C. We see, therefore, that the cost function is 'concave upwards'.

It is crucial to observe that the concavity of the cost function is quite independent of whether consumer preferences are assumed to be strictly convex or not. The cost function will be concave even for the indifference curves illustrated in Figs 2.2 and 2.3. This concavity means we are able to make use of the differential calculus without having to make the restrictive assumption of convex preferences.

The importance of the cost function lies in the fact that, if we start with equation [2.10], then *its differentiation with respect to p_1 and p_2 leads back to equations [2.8], the Hicksian compensated demand functions*. This property is generally referred to as *Shephard's lemma* (see, for example, Appendix B). The ordinary Marshallian demand functions can then be obtained by substituting for U^* in [2.8] using the indirect utility function [2.9].

As an illustration of the derivation of Hicksian and Marshallian demand equations from a cost function, let us return to the (strictly quasi-concave) utility function $U = q_1^2 q_2^3$ and the corresponding cost function [2.10A]:

$$m^* = \left(\frac{5}{2}\right)^{2/5}\left(\frac{5}{3}\right)^{3/5}(U^*)^{1/5}p_2^{3/5}p_1^{2/5}$$

Differentiation with respect to p_1 and p_2 yields

$$\frac{\partial m^*}{\partial p_1} = \left(\frac{5}{2}\right)^{-3/5}\left(\frac{5}{3}\right)^{3/5}(U^*)^{1/5}\left(\frac{p_2}{p_1}\right)^{3/5} = \left(\frac{2}{3}\right)^{3/5}(U^*)^{1/5}\left(\frac{p_2}{p_1}\right)^{3/5} = q_1$$

and

$$\frac{\partial m^*}{\partial p_2} = \left(\frac{5}{2}\right)^{2/5}\left(\frac{5}{3}\right)^{-2/5}(U^*)^{1/5}\left(\frac{p_1}{p_2}\right)^{2/5} = \left(\frac{2}{3}\right)^{-2/5}(U^*)^{1/5}\left(\frac{p_1}{p_2}\right)^{2/5} = q_2$$

These expressions are identical to the Hicksian demand equations [2.8A] obtained, more directly, by the minimisation of consumer costs. Finally, if we substitute for U^* in these functions using the indirect utility function [2.9A], we obtain again the Marshallian demand functions $q_1 = 2m/5p_1$ and $q_2 = 3m/5p_2$ derived on page 35.

Since the original utility function, $U = q_1^2 q_2^3$, was strictly quasi-concave, the Marshallian demands were more easily derived in this case by solving the utility maximising problem. However, we can now see one of the major advantages of working with the cost function rather than the underlying utility function. *Any cost function that possesses the properties listed above can be regarded as representative of some underlying consumer preference ordering.* Thus we can, if we wish, *start* from some appropriate functional form for the cost function and then generate both Hicksian and Marshallian demand equations, also with an explicit functional form, using the above method. Moreover, we do not have to assume strictly convex preferences for this procedure to be valid. In contrast, of course, generating specific demand equations using the traditional approach requires starting with a strictly quasi-concave utility function. As we shall see, one of the best known of recent demand models makes use of the cost function approach.

2.3 General restrictions on demand equations

We derive in this section a series of quite general restrictions on the form of demand equations. These restrictions are a consequence, firstly, of the consumer's budget constraint and, secondly, of the assumption of utility maximisation/cost minimisation. We begin by again considering the two-good case.

It is often possible to obtain considerable additional insight if, instead of considering the levels of demands, prices and total expenditure, we consider infinitesimal changes. For example, taking the total differentials of equations [2.3] and [2.5] yields

$$\left. \begin{aligned} \mathrm{d}q_1 &= \frac{\partial q_1}{\partial p_1}\,\mathrm{d}p_1 + \frac{\partial q_1}{\partial p_2}\,\mathrm{d}p_2 + \frac{\partial q_1}{\partial m}\,\mathrm{d}m \\ \mathrm{d}q_2 &= \frac{\partial q_2}{\partial p_1}\,\mathrm{d}p_1 + \frac{\partial q_2}{\partial p_2}\,\mathrm{d}p_2 + \frac{\partial q_2}{\partial m}\,\mathrm{d}m \end{aligned} \right\} \qquad [2.11]$$

$$\mathrm{d}\lambda = \frac{\partial \lambda}{\partial p_1}\,\mathrm{d}p_1 + \frac{\partial \lambda}{\partial p_2}\,\mathrm{d}p_2 + \frac{\partial \lambda}{\partial m}\,\mathrm{d}m \qquad [2.12]$$

It is helpful to regard equations [2.11] and [2.12] as giving the variables $\mathrm{d}q_1$, $\mathrm{d}q_2$ and $\mathrm{d}\lambda$ as linear functions of the changes in prices, $\mathrm{d}p_1$ and $\mathrm{d}p_2$, and the change in total expenditure dm, with 'coefficients' given by the partial derivatives $\partial q_1/\partial p_1$, $\partial q_1/\partial p_2$, etc. However, it must be remembered that these 'coefficients' are not constants or parameters and will themselves generally be functions of p_1, p_2 and m. The two equations [2.11] represent what is known as a 'differential demand equation system' – that is, it determines changes in demands rather than the demands themselves. From the empirical viewpoint these equations are of more interest than [2.12] since [2.12] concerns variables such as the change in the immeasurable λ. However, we shall make use of [2.12] later.

It is now possible to derive the first of a series of quite general restrictions on the 'coefficients' of the differential demand system [2.11] simply by partially differentiating the budget constraint [2.2] (reproduced below) with respect to p_1, p_2 and m in turn:

$$p_1 q_1 + p_2 q_2 = m$$

Differentiating partially with respect to m yields

$$p_1 \frac{\partial q_1}{\partial m} + p_2 \frac{\partial q_2}{\partial m} = 1 \qquad\qquad [2.13]$$

while differentiating partially with respect to p_1 and p_2 yields, respectively,

$$p_1 \frac{\partial q_1}{\partial p_1} + p_2 \frac{\partial q_2}{\partial p_1} = -q_1 \quad \text{and} \quad p_1 \frac{\partial q_1}{\partial p_2} + p_2 \frac{\partial q_2}{\partial p_2} = -q_2 \qquad [2.14]$$

Hence we see that the coefficients of the differential demand system [2.11] must satisfy the 'restrictions' given by equations [2.13] and [2.14]. These are known as the *aggregation restrictions* since they are derived from the fact that expenditures on the individual goods must 'add up' to total expenditure.[7] Notice that they are obtained without any reference to the utility function and must therefore hold whether the consumer is a utility maximiser or not.

Another property that arises solely from the budget constraint is that of *homogeneity*. Since, for example, a doubling of p_1, p_2 and m leaves the budget constraint [2.2] unchanged, it should have no effect on a consumer's choices. *Demand equations are therefore homogeneous of degree zero in prices and total expenditure.* There is an absence of what is commonly called 'money illusion'. To see what this implies for the differential demand equations [2.11], suppose both prices and total expenditure increase by the same proportion, α. That is,

$$\frac{dm}{m} = \frac{dp_1}{p_1} = \frac{dp_2}{p_2} = \alpha.$$

Since, given such equiproportionate changes, $dq_1 = dq_2 = 0$, we obtain, substituting the above relationships into [2.11],

$$\left.\begin{array}{l} p_1 \dfrac{\partial q_1}{\partial p_1} + p_2 \dfrac{\partial q_1}{\partial p_2} + m \dfrac{\partial q_1}{\partial m} = 0 \\[3mm] p_1 \dfrac{\partial q_2}{\partial p_1} + p_2 \dfrac{\partial q_2}{\partial p_2} + m \dfrac{\partial q_2}{\partial m} = 0 \end{array}\right\} \qquad [2.15]$$

Equations [2.15] further restrict the 'coefficients' of the differential equations [2.11]. For obvious reasons they are known as *homogeneity restrictions*.

The aggregation and homogeneity restrictions are properties of the budget constraint and are independent of whether the consumer is a utility maximiser. However, if we make the assumption of utility maximisation (or equivalently cost minimisation), it is possible to derive a series of further restrictions on the differential demand equations [2.11]. These may be derived either using the traditional neo-classical approach or by making use of the cost function. The former approach, unlike the latter, requires the assumption of strictly convex preferences. However, we shall consider it in detail, both for historical reasons and because of the insights it provides. We consider the more general cost function approach later.

Recall that the maximisation of the (strictly quasi-concave) utility function [2.1] subject to the budget constraint [2.2] led to the 'mini-system' of demand equations [2.3] and to the equation for the Lagrangian multiplier [2.5]. By taking the total differentials of equations [2.3] and [2.5], we obtained the differential demand equations [2.11] and also [2.12]. By differentiating the budget constraint [2.2] by m, p_1 and p_2, we derived the aggregation restrictions on the 'coefficients' of [2.11]. Now, by differentiating the optimality conditions [2.4] (which result from utility maximisation) we can derive further restrictions.

First, differentiating [2.4] with respect to m yields

$$U_{11} \frac{\partial q_1}{\partial m} + U_{12} \frac{\partial q_2}{\partial m} = p_1 \frac{\partial \lambda}{\partial m} \quad \text{and} \quad U_{21} \frac{\partial q_1}{\partial m} + U_{22} \frac{\partial q_2}{\partial m} = p_2 \frac{\partial \lambda}{\partial m} \quad [2.16]$$

Next, differentiating each optimality condition with respect to p_1 and p_2 in turn yields

$$\left. \begin{array}{l} U_{11} \dfrac{\partial q_1}{\partial p_1} + U_{12} \dfrac{\partial q_2}{\partial p_1} = \lambda + p_1 \dfrac{\partial \lambda}{\partial p_1} \quad \text{and} \quad U_{21} \dfrac{\partial q_1}{\partial p_1} + U_{22} \dfrac{\partial q_2}{\partial p_1} = p_2 \dfrac{\partial \lambda}{\partial p_1} \\[3ex] U_{11} \dfrac{\partial q_1}{\partial p_2} + U_{12} \dfrac{\partial q_2}{\partial p_2} = p_1 \dfrac{\partial \lambda}{\partial p_2} \quad \text{and} \quad U_{21} \dfrac{\partial q_1}{\partial p_2} + U_{22} \dfrac{\partial q_2}{\partial p_2} = \lambda + p_2 \dfrac{\partial \lambda}{\partial p_2} \end{array} \right\}$$
$$[2.17]$$

Equations [2.16] and [2.17] provide six further restrictions on the 'coefficients' of equations [2.11] and [2.12]. Unlike the aggregation restrictions [2.13] and [2.14], however, [2.16] and [2.17] involve immeasurable quantities such as the second-order partial derivatives of the utility function. To derive further restrictions on the differential demand system [2.11] it is necessary to treat equations [2.13], [2.14], [2.16] and [2.17] as a system of nine linear equations which can be solved for the nine 'coefficients' of equations [2.11] and [2.12]. This is most easily done in matrix terms since the nine-equation system can be written as

$$\begin{bmatrix} U_{11} & U_{12} & p_1 \\[2ex] U_{21} & U_{22} & p_2 \\[2ex] p_1 & p_2 & 0 \end{bmatrix} \begin{bmatrix} \dfrac{\partial q_1}{\partial m} & \dfrac{\partial q_1}{\partial p_1} & \dfrac{\partial q_1}{\partial p_2} \\[2ex] \dfrac{\partial q_2}{\partial m} & \dfrac{\partial q_2}{\partial p_1} & \dfrac{\partial q_2}{\partial p_2} \\[2ex] -\dfrac{\partial \lambda}{\partial m} & -\dfrac{\partial \lambda}{\partial p_1} & -\dfrac{\partial \lambda}{\partial p_2} \end{bmatrix} = \begin{bmatrix} 0 & \lambda & 0 \\[2ex] 0 & 0 & \lambda \\[2ex] 1 & -q_1 & -q_2 \end{bmatrix} \quad [2.18]$$

Equation [2.18] is a version of what Barten (1966) called the *fundamental matrix equation of consumer demand theory*. Its solution involves pre-multiplying by the inverse of the first matrix on the left-hand side, which is the so-called 'bordered Hessian matrix of second-order partials'. The straightforward but messy details of this procedure need not concern us but they in fact lead to the following solution for the nine 'coefficients' of equations [2.11] and [2.12].

$$\frac{\partial q_i}{\partial m} = \frac{1}{\phi}(p_1 U^{i1} + p_2 U^{i2}) \qquad i = 1, 2 \tag{2.19}$$

$$\frac{\partial q_i}{\partial p_j} = \lambda U^{ij} - \frac{\lambda}{\phi}(p_1 U^{i1} + p_2 U^{i2})(p_1 U^{j1} + p_2 U^{j2})$$
$$\qquad - \frac{1}{\phi} q_j(p_1 U^{i1} + p_2 U^{i2}) \qquad i = 1, 2; \ j = 1, 2 \tag{2.20}$$

$$\frac{\partial \lambda}{\partial p_j} = -\frac{\lambda}{\phi}(p_1 U^{j1} + p_2 U^{j2}) - \frac{1}{\phi} q_j \qquad j = 1, 2; \tag{2.21}$$

$$\frac{\partial \lambda}{\partial m} = \frac{1}{\phi} \tag{}$$

where U^{ij} is the ijth element of the inverse of the Hessian matrix of second-order partials[8] and ϕ is given by

$$\phi = p_1^2 U^{11} + p_1 p_2 U^{12} + p_2 p_1 U^{21} + p_2^2 U^{22}$$

These equations may be expressed in more interesting form by substituting $\partial \lambda / \partial m = 1/\phi$ into equations [2.19], yielding

$$\frac{\partial q_i}{\partial m} = \frac{\partial \lambda}{\partial m}(p_1 U^{i1} + p_2 U^{i2}) \qquad i = 1, 2$$

and then substituting for $(p_1 U^{i1} + p_2 U^{i2})$ and $(p_1 U^{j1} + p_2 U^{j2})$ in equations [2.21] and [2.20]. This yields

$$\frac{\partial \lambda}{\partial p_j} = -\lambda \frac{\partial q_j}{\partial m} - \frac{\partial \lambda}{\partial m} q_j \qquad j = 1, 2 \tag{2.22}$$

and

$$\frac{\partial q_i}{\partial p_j} = \lambda U^{ij} - \left(\frac{\lambda}{\partial \lambda / \partial m}\right)\left(\frac{\partial q_i}{\partial m} \frac{\partial q_j}{\partial m}\right) - q_j\left(\frac{\partial q_i}{\partial m}\right) \qquad i = 1, 2; \ j = 1, 2 \tag{2.23}$$

Equations [2.23] are the Slutsky equations. The last term, $-q_j(\partial q_i / \partial m)$, is the income effect, so that the first two terms on the right-hand side of [2.23] must represent the substitution effect (cross-substitution effect if $i \neq j$). That is

$$k_{ij} = \left(\frac{\partial q_i}{\partial p_j}\right)_{U=\text{const}} = \lambda U^{ij} - \left(\frac{\lambda}{\partial \lambda / \partial m}\right)\left(\frac{\partial q_i}{\partial m} \frac{\partial q_j}{\partial m}\right) = \frac{\partial q_i}{\partial p_j} + q_j\left(\frac{\partial q_i}{\partial m}\right) \tag{2.24}$$

Notice that the (total) substitution effect can be divided into two components. In the terminology first introduced by Houthakker (1960), the component λU^{ij} is referred to as the *specific substitution effect* and the component

$-\left(\dfrac{\lambda}{\partial\lambda/\partial m}\right)\left(\dfrac{\partial q_i}{\partial m}\dfrac{\partial q_j}{\partial m}\right)$ as the *general substitution effect*. The meaning of these effects and the reasons for this terminology will be explained later. Notice, for the moment, that whereas the total substitution effect is measurable in the same sense that the price and income derivatives are, and is hence invariant under non-linear transformations of the utility function, the same cannot be said of its two components since they are dependent on various utility terms.

The remaining general restrictions on the 'coefficients' of the differential demand system [2.11] may now be obtained from the Slutsky equations. Firstly, we have the so-called *symmetry restriction* which refers to the cross-substitution effects. Since the Hessian matrix of second-order partials is symmetric, so must be its inverse. That is, since $U_{12} = U_{21}$ we have $U^{12} = U^{21}$ and it then follows from [2.24] that $k_{ij} = k_{ji}$, so that we may write

$$\frac{\partial q_1}{\partial p_2} + q_2 \frac{\partial q_1}{\partial m} = \frac{\partial q_2}{\partial p_1} + q_1 \frac{\partial q_2}{\partial m} \qquad [2.25]$$

Equation [2.25] implies that the (total) substitution effect of a unit change in p_2 on q_1 is identical to the (total) substitution effect of a unit change in p_1 on q_2.

Finally, we have the so-called *negativity restrictions* which refer to the 'own-substitution' effect on the demand for a good of a change in its own price. From equation [2.24] the effects are, for goods 1 and 2, respectively

$$k_{11} = \lambda U^{11} - \left(\frac{\lambda}{\partial\lambda/\partial m}\right)\left(\frac{\partial q_1}{\partial m}\right)^2 \quad \text{and} \quad k_{22} = \lambda U^{22} - \left(\frac{\lambda}{\partial\lambda/\partial m}\right)\left(\frac{\partial q_2}{\partial m}\right)^2 \qquad [2.26]$$

The reader will be familiar with the fact that $k_{11} < 0$ and $k_{22} < 0$. This is the famous 'law of demand' and implies that demand for a good always falls in response to a price rise which is accompanied by a compensating payment which maintains utility intact. In the present approach it follows from a combination of the fundamental equation [2.18] with the fact that U_{11} and U_{22} and hence U^{11} and U^{22} are both negative.[9]

Notice at this point that it is possible to derive the homogeneity restrictions [2.15] obtained earlier by combining the aggregation restrictions, [2.13] and [2.14] and the symmetry restriction [2.35]. For example, combining [2.13] with the first equation in [2.14] yields

$$p_1 \frac{\partial q_1}{\partial p_1} + p_2 \frac{\partial q_2}{\partial p_1} = -q_1\left(p_1 \frac{\partial q_1}{\partial m} + p_2 \frac{\partial q_2}{\partial m}\right)$$

or

$$p_1\left(\frac{\partial q_1}{\partial p_1} + q_1 \frac{\partial q_1}{\partial m}\right) + p_2\left(\frac{\partial q_2}{\partial p_1} + q_1 \frac{\partial q_2}{\partial m}\right) = 0$$

Hence, using the symmetry restriction [2.25] and the fact that $p_1 q_1 + p_2 q_2 = m$, we have

$$p_1 \frac{\partial q_1}{\partial p_1} + p_2 \frac{\partial q_1}{\partial p_2} + m \frac{\partial q_1}{\partial m} = 0$$

This, of course, is identical to the first of equations [2.15]. Similarly, the second of equations [2.15] can be obtained by combining [2.13] with the second of equations [2.14] and then using the symmetry restriction. As we have seen, the property of homogeneity is more easily deduced simply by considering the budget constraint. However, the above derivation illustrates the point that *the aggregation, symmetry and homogeneity restrictions are not independent of one another.* If demand equations satisfy the aggregation and symmetry restrictions they will automatically satisfy the homogeneity restrictions. However, satisfaction of the homogeneity and aggregation restrictions does not necessarily imply that the symmetry restriction will be satisfied. Symmetry is therefore said to be a 'stronger' restriction than homogeneity. It, in fact, reflects consistency of consumer choice, whereas homogeneity merely reflects the consumer's budget constraint.

We have now exhausted all the general restrictions on the equation system [2.11] that can be derived from neo-classical consumer theory. It may seem that we have not made all the use we might of the matrix equation [2.18] – for example, as yet we have found no use at all for equation [2.22]. Indeed, further restrictions on the 'coefficients' of equations [2.11] and [2.12] can be derived, but these invariably involve the 'coefficients' of the 'unobservable' equation [2.12] and are therefore of little interest from the empirical point of view.

The cost function approach

It must be stressed at this point that our derivations of the properties of symmetry and negativity depend crucially on the initial assumption of strictly convex preferences and a strictly quasi-concave utility function. Without such a utility function the Lagrangian multiplier approach is not feasible. Moreover, it is this property of the utility function that ensures that U^{11} and U^{22} in equation [2.26] are negative. Hence, it is the assumption of strict quasi-concavity which, in the above derivation, ensures the negativity of the own-price substitution effect. This raises the interesting question of whether the famous 'law of demand' would hold if preferences were non-convex. The best way of answering this question is by approaching the problem via the cost function introduced earlier.

The property of symmetry is easily derived using the cost function if we recall that its differentiation with respect to p_1 and p_2 leads back to the Hicksian compensated demand functions [2.8]. That is,

$$\frac{\partial m}{\partial p_1} = f_1(p_1, p_2, U^*) \quad \text{and} \quad \frac{\partial m}{\partial p_2} = f_2(p_1, p_2, U^*) \qquad [2.27]$$

Differentiating the first of the above equations by p_2 and the second by p_1 yields

$$\frac{\partial^2 m}{\partial p_1 \, \partial p_2} = \frac{\partial f_1}{\partial p_2} \quad \text{and} \quad \frac{\partial^2 m}{\partial p_2 \, \partial p_1} = \frac{\partial f_2}{\partial p_1}$$

Since the cost function is necessarily concave, it must have continuous derivatives. Young's theorem therefore holds and we have

$$\frac{\partial^2 m}{\partial p_1 \, \partial p_2} = \frac{\partial^2 m}{\partial p_2 \, \partial p_1} \quad \text{and hence} \quad \frac{\partial f_1}{\partial p_2} = \frac{\partial f_2}{\partial p_1}.$$

That is, the derivative of the first Hicksian demand with respect to the second price equals the derivative of the second Hicksian demand with respect to the first price. However, the price derivatives of the Hicksian demand functions measure the effects on demand of a change in price when consumer utility is held constant. That is, the cross-derivatives measure the (total) cross-substitution effects. Thus by deriving the equation $\partial f_1/\partial p_2 = \partial f_2/\partial p_1$ we have derived the symmetry property of demand equations. Moreover, this derivation is independent of whether preferences are assumed to be strictly convex or not, because in either case the cost function is concave.

The property of negativity is a direct consequence of the concavity of the cost function. Concavity implies that the second-order derivatives of the cost function, $\partial^2 m/\partial p_1^2$ and $\partial^2 m/\partial p_2^2$ are both negative. Moreover, from [2.27]

$$\frac{\partial^2 m}{\partial p_1^2} = \frac{\partial f_1}{\partial p_1} \quad \text{and} \quad \frac{\partial^2 m}{\partial p_2^2} = \frac{\partial f_2}{\partial p_2}$$

Hence, concavity of the cost function implies that the own-price derivatives of the Hicksian demand functions must be negative. These own-price derivatives are, of course, the own-price (total) substitution effects. Thus we have derived the property of negativity, and as with symmetry the derivation is independent of any assumption of strictly convex preferences. The cost function is concave whether or not preferences are strictly convex.

Since the concavity of the cost function is a direct consequence of the fact that the consumer is a utility maximiser/cost minimiser, the above derivation well illustrates the fact that negativity is a reflection of the assumption of utility maximisation. We may therefore close this discussion by noting that of the general restrictions on demand equations, the aggregation and homogeneity restrictions reflect the consumer's budget constraint, whereas the symmetry and negativity restrictions reflect consistency of consumer choice.

The general n-good case

All the above restrictions carry over into the general case where the consumer purchases n goods. The demand system [2.3] then consists of n equations

$$q_i = q_i(p_1, p_2, p_3, \ldots, p_n, m) \qquad i = 1, 2, 3, \ldots, n \qquad \text{[2.3A]}$$

where q_i and p_i are the demand and price, respectively, of the ith good and total expenditure $m = \Sigma p_i q_i$.

Alternatively, in terms of infinitesimal changes we have the differential demand system

$$\mathrm{d}q_i = \sum_j \frac{\partial q_i}{\partial p_j} \mathrm{d}p_j + \frac{\partial q_i}{\partial m} \mathrm{d}m \qquad i = 1, 2, 3, \ldots, n \qquad \text{[2.11A]}$$

In the general case, the aggregation restrictions become

$$\sum_i p_i \frac{\partial q_i}{\partial m} = 1 \qquad \text{[2.13A]}$$

and

$$\sum_i p_i \frac{\partial q_i}{\partial p_j} = -q_j \qquad j = 1, 2, 3, \ldots, n \qquad \text{[2.14A]}$$

The symmetry restriction becomes

$$k_{ij} = \frac{\partial q_i}{\mathrm{d}p_j} + q_j \frac{\partial q_i}{\partial m} = \frac{\partial q_j}{\partial p_i} + q_i \frac{\partial q_j}{\partial m} = k_{ji} \qquad \text{all } i \neq j \qquad [2.25\text{A}]$$

Just as in the two-good case the homogeneity restriction may be derived either from the budget constraint or from a combination of the aggregation and symmetry restrictions. In the general case,

$$\sum_j p_j \frac{\partial q_i}{\partial p_j} + m \frac{\partial q_i}{\partial m} = 0 \qquad i = 1, 2, 3, \ldots, n \qquad [2.15\text{A}]$$

However, the aggregation and homogeneity restrictions do not necessarily imply symmetry, so again we see that symmetry is a 'stronger' restriction than homogeneity. Finally, we have the negativity restrictions which in the general case are

$$k_{ii} = \frac{\partial q_i}{\partial p_i} + q_i \frac{\partial q_i}{\partial m} = \lambda U^{ii} - \left(\frac{\lambda}{\partial \lambda / \partial m} \right) \left(\frac{\partial q_i}{\partial m} \right)^2 < 0 \qquad i = 1, 2, 3, \ldots, n$$
$$[2.26\text{A}]$$

Notice that, of the general restrictions, those of aggregation and symmetry are *cross-equation* restrictions, requiring the estimation of the complete system [2.3A] or [2.11A] before they can be tested for or enforced. If attention is concentrated on a single equation, the only restrictions that can be made use of are those of homogeneity and negativity.

All the above restrictions have been formulated in terms of the 'coefficients' of the differential demand system [2.11A]. Such a formulation might be convenient if we wished to 'parametrise' these quantities, i.e. treat them as unknown constants ignoring their general theoretical dependence on all prices and total expenditure. We could then attempt the estimation of either a linear version of the system [2.3A]

$$q_i = \alpha_{i0} + \alpha_{i1}p_1 + \alpha_{i2}p_2 + \cdots + \alpha_{in}p_n + \alpha_{im}m \qquad i = 1, 2, 3, \ldots, n$$
$$[2.28]$$

or a version of [2.11A] in which infinitesimal changes are replaced by, for example, finite quarterly or annual changes

$$\Delta q_i = \alpha_{i1}\Delta p_1 + \alpha_{i2} \Delta p_2 + \cdots + \alpha_{in} \Delta p_n + \alpha_{im}\Delta m \qquad i = 1, 2, 3, \ldots, n$$
$$[2.29]$$

where $\alpha_{ij} = \partial q_i / \partial p_j$ for all i and j, and $\alpha_{im} = \partial q_i / \partial m$ for all i, are the 'parameters' being estimated.

Some alternative parametrisations
The general restrictions, however, can be reformulated in various ways, depending on what quantity or concept the investigator wishes to parametrise. For example, a frequently adopted approach is to treat elasticities rather than partial derivatives as constants and estimate double logarithmic systems of the form

$$q_i = A_i p_1^{\varepsilon_{i1}} p_2^{\varepsilon_{i2}} p_3^{\varepsilon_{i3}} \ldots p_n^{\varepsilon_{in}} m^{\eta_i} \qquad i = 1, 2, 3, \ldots, n \qquad [2.30]$$

where ε_{ij} is the elasticity of demand for the ith good with respect to the jth price and η_i is the total expenditure elasticity of the ith good.

The restrictions can be rewritten in terms of elasticities as follows. Considering the aggregation restrictions first, equation [2.13A] may be written as

$$\sum_i w_i \eta_i = 1 \qquad \qquad [2.13B]$$

where $w_i = p_i q_i / m$ is the 'budget share' of the ith good, i.e. the proportion of total expenditure spent on that good. Similarly, equations [2.14A] can be rewritten as

$$\sum_i w_i \varepsilon_{ij} = -w_j \qquad j = 1, 2, 3, \cdots, n \qquad \qquad [2.14B]$$

The symmetry restrictions [2.25A] become

$$w_i(\varepsilon_{ij} + \eta_i w_j) = w_j(\varepsilon_{ji} + \eta_j w_i) \qquad \text{all } i \neq j \qquad \qquad [2.25B]$$

The homogeneity restrictions [2.15A] become

$$\sum_j \varepsilon_{ij} + \eta_i = 0 \qquad i = 1, 2, 3, \ldots, n \qquad \qquad [2.15B]$$

That is, for each good the sum of the price elasticities and the income elasticity must be zero. Finally the negativity restrictions [2.26A] become

$$w_i(\varepsilon_{ii} + \eta_i w_i) < 0 \qquad i = 1, 2, 3, \ldots, n \qquad \qquad [2.26B]$$

It may now seem that we are fully equipped to enforce the general restrictions of theory on demand systems and reap the benefits of constrained or restricted estimation mentioned at the outset. Alternatively, why not estimate such systems in unrestricted form and thereby 'test' the validity of the restrictions implied by consumer theory? Unfortunately there is one rather serious difficulty. Whether the restrictions are formulated in first derivative or elasticity form, their precise form is dependent on the prevailing levels of prices and total expenditure. For example, if the income derivatives are treated as constants then the form of restriction [2.13A] will depend on the levels of prices. This means that for any of the systems [2.28], [2.29] or [2.30] to be fully consistent with consumer theory (i.e. consistent at all possible configurations of prices and total expenditure) they must satisfy an infinite number of restrictions. This is clearly not feasible. Thus, it *is not possible for such systems to fully satisfy all the general restrictions*. For example, if goods have constant income elasticities as in system [2.30], then as income rises, the proportion of expenditure that goes on goods with high income elasticities must increase so that $\Sigma_i w_i \eta_i$ must increase. However, this is inconsistent with the aggregation restriction [2.13B] which states that $\Sigma_i w_i \eta_i$ should in fact always equal unity.

The above difficulties obviously limit the usefulness of demand systems such as [2.28], [2.29] and [2.30]. In practice, if the general restrictions are to be imposed they have to be imposed in such a way that they hold exactly only at pre-specified levels of prices and total expenditure – for example, at the point of sample means. Alternatively, the systems can be estimated without any restrictions imposed and then a check made to see whether they satisfy the restrictions at the point of sample means.

Clearly it would be most useful if we could develop demand systems for which the general restrictions of theory remain unchanged for all possible levels of prices and total expenditure. In fact we can derive one such system if we employ as dependent variables, not the quantities demanded, q_i, but variables of the form $w_i(dq_i/q_i) = w_i \, d \log q_i$. This may, at first, seem a peculiar choice for the role of dependent variable. However, it must be remembered that consumer theory is essentially a theory about the *allocation* of total expenditure between various goods. We ought, therefore, perhaps, to be considering $w_i = p_i q_i/m$, the proportion allocated to good i, rather than q_i, the quantity demanded. The budget share w_i will change as total expenditure m and price p_i change, both directly because it depends on these variables and indirectly since the consumer adjusts q_i in response to changes in m and p_i. More precisely

$$
dw_i = \left(\frac{p_i}{m}\right) dq_i + \left(\frac{q_i}{m}\right) dp_i - \left(\frac{p_i q_i}{m^2}\right) dm
$$

$$
= w_i\left(\frac{dq_i}{q_i}\right) + w_i\left(\frac{dp_i}{p_i}\right) - w_i\left(\frac{dm}{m}\right)
$$

or

$$
dw_i = w_i \, d \log q_i + w_i \, d \log p_i - w_i \, d \log m \qquad [2.31]
$$

Since the consumer takes changes in prices and total expenditure as given, it is only the first term on the right-hand side of equation [2.31] which is endogenously determined and this makes $w_i \, d \log q_i$ a very suitable choice as dependent variable. Since $w_i \, d \log q_i = (p_i/m) \, dq_i$ we can obtain a demand system with such dependent variables by multiplying equations [2.11A] throughout by p_i/m. After considerable manipulation, this leads eventually to equations of the form

$$
w_i \, d \log q_i = \sum_j \pi_{ij} \, d \log p_j + \mu_i \sum_i w_i \, d \log q_i \qquad i = 1, 2, 3, \ldots, n
$$

$$
[2.32]
$$

where

$$
\mu_i = p_i \frac{\partial q_i}{\partial m} = \frac{\partial(p_i q_i)}{\partial m}
$$

is the 'marginal budget share' of good i or the marginal propensity to consume that good, and

$$
\pi_{ij} = \frac{p_i p_j}{m} k_{ij} = w_i\left(\frac{p_j}{q_i}\right) k_{ij}
$$

is the 'compensated' elasticity of the ith good with respect to the jth price multiplied by the budget share of the ith good. Notice that both the μ_i and the π_{ij} will generally be dependent on total expenditure m and on all prices. The influence of changes in expenditure on the change in budget share is reflected in equation [2.32] by the term $\Sigma \, w_i \, d \log q_i$ which is a measure of the change in real income.

The differential demand system [2.32] is the basis of the *Rotterdam* model first presented by Theil (1965). The great attraction of this system is that, provided one is prepared to treat the μ_i and π_{ij} as constants, ignoring their general dependence on total expenditure and prices, the restrictions of consumer theory, when applied to equation [2.32] are *unchanged for all values of total expenditure and prices.* In fact, this system, unlike [2.28], [2.29] and [2.30] is capable of satisfying all these restrictions exactly and, moreover, of doing so at all points. In terms of the μ_i and the π_{ij}, the aggregation restrictions become, from [2.13A]

$$\sum_i \mu_i = 1 \qquad\qquad [2.13C]$$

and since

$$\sum_i \pi_{ij} = \sum_i \frac{p_i p_j}{m} \left(\frac{\partial q_i}{\partial p_j} + q_j \frac{\partial q_i}{\partial m} \right)$$

$$= \frac{p_j}{m} \sum_i p_i \frac{\partial q_i}{\partial p_j} + \frac{p_j q_j}{m} \sum_i p_i \frac{\partial q_i}{\partial m}$$

it follows, using equations [2.13A] and [2.14A] that

$$\sum_i \pi_{ij} = 0 \qquad j = 1, 2, 3, \ldots, n \qquad [2.14C]$$

The symmetry restrictions [2.25A] become

$$\pi_{ij} = \pi_{ji} \qquad \text{all } i \neq j, \qquad\qquad [2.25C]$$

the homogeneity restrictions [2.15A] become

$$\sum_j \pi_{ij} = 0 \qquad i = 1, 2, 3, \ldots, n \qquad [2.15C]$$

and finally the negativity restrictions [2.26A] become

$$\pi_{ii} < 0 \qquad i = 1, 2, 3, \ldots, n \qquad [2.26C]$$

Notice that the strongest of these restrictions, [2.13C], [2.14C] and [2.25C] are all of particularly simple linear form and this makes it easier both to impose them prior to the estimation process and to test for their validity. However, there are dangers in arbitrarily selecting certain quantities, 'parametrising' them and ignoring their theoretical dependence on total expenditure and prices. A demand system such as [2.32] may appear completely general and capable of arising out of any specific type of underlying utility function. Unfortunately, we shall see later that arbitrary parametrisation can have unexpected and sometimes wholly unacceptable implications for the form of that utility function.

It should now be clear that if it proves both justifiable and possible to impose the general restrictions on a demand system, there will be a large reduction in the number of independent parameters which have to be estimated. For example, in an n-equation system without restrictions there will be $n^2 + n$ parameters, reflecting n^2 responses to price changes (e.g. the π_{ij} in the Rotterdam model) and n responses to income changes (e.g. the μ_i in the Rotterdam model). The aggregation restrictions reduce the number of inde-pendent responses by $n + 1$ (e.g. if $n - 1$ of the μ_i's are known, the nth may be calculated as one minus the sum of the others using [2.13C]. The symmetry restrictions reduce the number by a further $\frac{1}{2}n(n - 1)$, (e.g. once π_{37} has been estimated we also have an estimate of π_{73}). Hence, ignoring the weaker negativity restrictions the number of independent responses can be reduced to

$$n^2 + n - (n + 1) - \tfrac{1}{2}n(n - 1) = \tfrac{1}{2}n(n + 1) - 1 \qquad [2.33]$$

Thus in a 10-equation system, for example, the number of independent responses is reduced from 110 to 54.

Unfortunately, given the limited spans of data that are normally available, 54 parameters is still likely to be far too many for their joint estimation. For this reason, in practice it is frequently found necessary to impose further restrictions on the form of demand systems.

These additional restrictions are obtained by making particular assumptions about the precise form of the utility function and about the structure of consumer preferences. However, before we consider these additional 'particular restrictions' it will be useful to examine in greater depth the division, in equation [2.23], of the total substitution effect into its specific and general components.

2.4   The general and specific substitution effects

In the general n-good case, equation [2.23], derived under the assumption of convex preferences, becomes

$$\frac{\partial q_i}{\partial p_j} = \lambda U^{ij} - \left(\frac{\lambda}{\partial \lambda / \partial m} \right) \left(\frac{\partial q_i}{\partial m} \frac{\partial q_j}{\partial m} \right) - q_j \frac{\partial q_i}{\partial m}$$

$$i = 1, 2, \ldots, n \quad j = 1, 2, \ldots, n \qquad [2.34]$$

where U^{ij} is, again, the ijth element in the inverse of what is now the $n \times n$ Hessian matrix of second-order partial derivatives of the utility function.

The reader will be aware that the term, $q_j(\partial q_i / \partial m)$, represents the income effect on q_i of a change in the jth price – that is, it reflects the influence on q_i of the changed purchasing power that results from a unit change in p_j. The remaining two terms on the right-hand side of equation [2.34] must therefore represent the total substitution effect or 'income compensated' effect of a change in the jth price. For the sake of completeness we shall derive this result analytically.

If the jth price rises by $\mathrm{d}p_j$, all other prices remaining unchanged, but the consumer simultaneously receives a compensating payment of $\mathrm{d}m = q_j \, \mathrm{d}p_j$ which enables him to buy the original basket of goods (and to retain his original utility level), then using equation [2.11A], the change in demand for the ith good will be

$$\mathrm{d}q_i = \frac{\partial q_i}{\partial p_j} \, \mathrm{d}p_j + \frac{\partial q_i}{\partial m} \, q_j \, \mathrm{d}p_j$$

and hence, using equation [2.34],

$$\left(\frac{\partial q_i}{\partial p_j} \right)_{U=\mathrm{const}} = \frac{\partial q_i}{\partial p_j} + \frac{\partial q_i}{\partial m} q_j = \lambda U^{ij} - \left(\frac{\lambda}{\partial \lambda / \partial m} \right) \left(\frac{\partial q_i}{\partial m} \frac{\partial q_j}{\partial m} \right) \qquad [2.35]$$

When the price of good j changes, the marginal utility of total expenditure, λ, also changes, since λ is a function of m and all prices. Suppose, for a reason to be made clearer later, when p_j changes we consider the compensating payment

52

required not to keep total utility constant but to keep the marginal utility of total expenditure, λ, constant. For price change dp_j and total expenditure change dm, the change in λ is, using the general case version of equation [2.12],

$$d\lambda = \frac{\partial \lambda}{\partial m} dm + \frac{\partial \lambda}{\partial p_j} dp_j = \frac{\partial \lambda}{\partial m} dm - \left(\lambda \frac{\partial q_j}{\partial m} + \frac{\partial \lambda}{\partial m} q_j \right) dp_j \qquad [2.36]$$

where the substitution for $\partial \lambda / \partial p_j$ is based on the general case version of equation [2.22].

Hence if λ is to be held constant, i.e. if $d\lambda = 0$, from [2.36] the compensating payment required is

$$dm = q_j \, dp_j + \left(\frac{\lambda}{\partial \lambda / \partial m} \right) \frac{\partial q_j}{\partial m} dp_j \qquad [2.37]$$

Thus, if the consumer faces a price change dp_j and simultaneously receives the compensating payment given by equation [2.37] then, again using equation [2.11A], the change in demand for the ith good will be

$$dq_i = \frac{\partial q_i}{\partial p_j} dp_j + \frac{\partial q_i}{\partial m} \left[q_j \, dp_j + \left(\frac{\lambda}{\partial \lambda / \partial m} \right) \frac{\partial q_j}{\partial m} dp_j \right]$$

and hence

$$\left(\frac{\partial q_i}{\partial p_j} \right)_{\lambda = \text{const}} = \frac{\partial q_i}{\partial p_j} + q_j \frac{\partial q_i}{\partial m} + \left(\frac{\lambda}{\partial \lambda / \partial m} \right) \left(\frac{\partial q_i}{\partial m} \frac{\partial q_j}{\partial m} \right) = \lambda U^{ij} \qquad [2.38]$$

where the final step is based on equation [2.34]. Thus the component λU^{ij} in equation [2.34] measures the effect on q_i of a change in p_j when the consumer is compensated in such a way as to leave the marginal utility of total expenditure unchanged.

To see why we should be interested in a compensating payment which maintains λ constant and to understand the economic significance, firstly of the term λU^{ij} in equation [2.34] and, secondly, of the term $\left(\dfrac{\lambda}{\delta \lambda / \delta m} \right) \left(\dfrac{\partial q_i}{\delta m} \dfrac{\partial q_j}{\delta m} \right)$

which is the remaining component of the total substitution effect, we need to interpret further the Lagrangian multiplier λ.

In one sense λ measures the extent to which the consumer's choices, as he seeks to maximise utility, are influenced or constrained by his overall budget equation. For example, suppose that, in the absence of the constraint that total expenditure cannot exceed some given value, the utility maximising choices of the consumer were such that total expenditure was anyway less than or equal to that given value. The imposition of the constraint would thus have no effect on consumer choices and the value of λ, the marginal utility of total expenditure, would be zero. This is because in such a situation an increase in m has no effect on choices and hence leads to no increase in utility. More generally, the greater the extent to which the consumer's unconstrained choices would result in a total expenditure greater than the permitted level (i.e. that the existence of the budget constraint actually restricts choice), the larger will be the size of λ. Hence the greater will be the increase in utility resulting from a unit increase in total expenditure.

There are two ways in which any pair of goods can be regarded as being in competition with one another for a consumer's expenditure. Firstly, a compensated (so as to keep total utility constant) change in the price of good j will affect the consumer's demand for good i to the extent that the goods are related by taste. The size of this effect will be dependent on the form of the consumer's (cardinal) utility function, e.g. on the extent to which U_{ij} differs from zero.[10] Our *a priori* knowledge of the degree to which goods are 'substitutes' or 'complements' refers to this effect. Secondly, however, all goods compete for the consumer's expenditure in a *general* sense, since, because of the existence of the budget constraint, q_j cannot be increased unless it is at the expense of purchases of some or all of the other goods (including good i). Hence a compensated change in p_j can affect the demand for good i both because of the specific relationship in terms of taste between the two goods, and because any change in q_j must have a general effect on the demand for all goods, including good i. The first of these effects is known as the *specific* substitution effect and the second as the *general* substitution effect. When the consumer is compensated for a price change dp_j by a payment sufficient to maintain λ constant, we are in fact eliminating the general component of the total substitution effect, since by keeping λ constant we maintain unchanged the extent to which choices are constrained by the budget equation. If λ were to vary as a consequence of the change in p_j this would signal the operation of a general substitution effect. Since compensating so as to maintain λ constant leads to the elimination of the general effect and also, from equation [2.38], reduces the total substitution effect to λU^{ij}, it is the quantity λU^{ij} which must represent the specific substitution effect on q_i of a change in p_j. The quantity $\left(\dfrac{-\lambda}{\partial \lambda / \partial m} \right) \left(\dfrac{\partial q_i}{\partial m} \dfrac{\partial q_j}{\partial m} \right)$ represents the general substitution effect.

Notice, however, that whereas the total substitution effect can be expressed in terms of measurable quantities (viz $\partial q_i / \partial p_j + q_j (\partial q_i / \partial m)$ and is invariant under monotonic transformations of the utility function, the same cannot be said about the sizes of the specific and general substitution effects. These depend on immeasurable quantities such as λ and U^{ij}. It is therefore difficult to give an ordinal interpretation to these concepts, although we shall see later that the absence of a specific cross-substitution effect (which occurs when $U^{ij} = 0$ for some $i \neq j$) does have an observable analogue.

Notice also that our discussion of the general and specific substitution effects has been based on equation [2.34]. However, equation [2.34] is only derivable if we follow the traditional neo-classical approach to consumer theory and hence requires the assumption of strictly convex preferences. This is not to say that the total substitution effect cannot be split into general and specific components when preferences are non-convex. Intuitively, it should be clear that goods can compete with each other both in a specific taste-related way and in a general way, whether preferences are strictly convex or not. However, if preferences are not strictly convex then we cannot make use of the precise expressions just derived for the specific and general effects.

Substitutes and complements

The old 'cardinalist' definitions of substitutability and complementarity were based on the sign of the second-order cross-partial derivatives of the utility function. For example, if $U_{ij} < 0$, this implied substitutability since an increase in the consumption of good j reduces the marginal utility of good i. These definitions had the advantage of corresponding to intuitive concepts of substitutability and complementarity but the disadvantage that the signs of the second-order derivatives were not invariant under non-linear transformations of the utility function.

The 'ordinalist' or Hicksian definitions make use of the fact that the signs of the total cross-substitution effects (i.e. the k_{ij} in equation [2.25A]) are invariant under non-linear transformations. Thus in Hicksian terms, two goods are substitutes when $k_{ij} > 0$, i.e. if when the price of one good rises, the consumer who has received a compensating payment purchases more of the other. Similarly, if $k_{ij} < 0$, the two goods are Hicksian complements. However, the Hicksian definitions also suffer from disadvantages. It is well known that they are 'biased in favour of substitutability' in the sense that it is possible for all goods to be substitutes but not possible for all goods to be complements. Moreover, they can also lead to apparent paradoxes and contradictions. Consider the following.

Suppose two goods are 'want independent' in the sense that a change in the consumption of one good does not affect the marginal utility of consuming the other. This implies that $U_{ij} = U_{ji} = 0$ and hence that $U^{ij} = U^{ji} = 0$. Specific cross-substitution effects are therefore zero, so that the total substitution effect reduces to its general component. That is, using [2.24]

$$k_{ij} = -\left(\frac{\lambda}{\partial\lambda/\partial m}\right)\left(\frac{\partial q_i}{\partial m}\frac{\partial q_j}{\partial m}\right).$$

Thus, since $\lambda > 0$ and $\partial\lambda/\partial m < 0$, if the income derivatives are positive (and we shall see later that want independence implies that they must be) we have $k_{ij} > 0$. Thus when goods are completely unrelated from the point of view of taste they are still substitutes under the Hicksian definitions.

The decomposition of the total substitution effect into its specific and general components goes some way towards resolving these apparent contradictions. In the above case, for example, the Hicksian substitutability referred to simply reflects the fact that all goods compete in a general sense for the consumer's expenditure. Goods are *specific* substitutes only if $U^{ij} > 0$. The difficulty, of course, is that the sign of the specific substitution effect is not invariant under non-linear transformations of the utility function. However, attempts have more recently been made (e.g. Barten 1971) to combine the intuitive appeal of the cardinalist definitions with the invariance property of the ordinalist or Hicksian ones.

2.5 Applying the model to existing data

The theoretical model of the previous subsections refers to the individual consumer, whereas available data are almost invariably of an aggregate nature. That is, they refer to the combined expenditures of many consumers. This raises two questions, the first of which we have already touched on when considering the estimation of single demand equations. This concerns whether or not there exist functions which give aggregate demands as stable functions of (relative) prices and aggregate (real) total expenditure. The second concerns whether, given that such stable functions exist, they can be expected to satisfy restrictions derived from a theory that relates to a single consumer. Only if the answers to both these questions are in the affirmative is it legitimate either to impose these restrictions on demand equations estimated from aggregate data or to use such data to test their validity.

We shall consider the problem of aggregating over consumers shortly. However, even if we had data on an individual consumer who was in some sense so 'representative' that we could regard his responses as being typical of consumers in general, we would still face serious problems in estimating a system of demand equations for such a person. The consumer is faced with a multitude of goods between which total expenditure has to be allocated. In attempting to estimate demand equations for every such commodity we would face insuperable problems over degrees of freedom even were we able to utilise all the general restrictions derivable from consumer theory. There are a number of interrelated ways by which we can attempt to get round this problem.

(a) It is possible to make assumptions concerning the precise form of the consumer's utility function which result in *particular restrictions* on demand equations far stronger than the general restrictions of unaided theory. In this manner the number of independent price and total expenditure responses that have to be handled can be drastically reduced. The most frequently used of these assumptions will be described in a moment.

(b) It may be possible to aggregate over certain groups of goods in such a way that we can treat these groups as if they were single *composite commodities*. In practice this is likely to be necessary anyway since available data tend to refer to broad aggregate groupings such as 'food', 'clothing', 'entertainment', etc.

(c) It may be possible to *represent* the consumer's overall allocation problem by a series of two or more 'stages' which may then be considered sequentially. This involves the idea of what is known as *multi-stage budgeting*. In the simplest case – known as two-stage budgeting – the consumer is envisaged as firstly determining the allocation of his total expenditure between various broad commodity groupings, e.g. 'food', 'clothing', etc. The only information used at this 'stage' is the size of total expenditure and appropriately defined price indices for the various groupings. At the second 'stage' the consumer decides for each grouping how the already determined group-expenditure should be allocated between the various goods in the grouping. Only at this stage is information on the prices of individual goods required and in deciding on the allocations within each group *use is made only of the prices of goods within that group*. Notice that if it is to be possible to represent the overall problem in this way a necessary condition is that we should be able to form the composite commodities envisaged in (b) above.

We have already implicitly used a two-stage budgeting approach in the model of consumer behaviour described in Section 2.1. There it was implicitly assumed that total expenditure, m, was predetermined in some way. However, the full problem faced by a consumer is that of allocating his total life-time resources between the purchasing of many different goods today and their purchase at various times in the future. We in fact assumed that the consumer proceeded in two stages: firstly, deciding on that part of his total resources that was to be devoted to current expenditure and, secondly, once total expenditure had been determined, deciding on its allocation between individual commodities.

Clearly it might be convenient, if possible, to take this procedure several steps further. Once the consumer has decided on total current expenditure he could next be regarded as determining its allocation between various broad commodity groupings such as 'food' or 'clothing'. Next, each total group expenditure could be regarded as being allocated to various subgroups of goods within the broad group. For example, total food expenditure might be allocated to 'meat', 'fruit', etc. Finally, once the subgroup expenditures had been decided on, their allocation to actual individual goods within each subgroup would be determined. Data, however, are, to a lesser or greater extent, normally aggregate in nature. Ideally we would therefore like it to be possible to arrange the stages in the representation[11] of the consumer's overall problem in such a way that either the broad groupings or the subgroupings of commodities correspond to actual available data series. Part of a multi-stage decision-making process is illustrated diagrammatically in Fig. 2.5.

At this point it should be emphasised that it is by no means certain that the consumer's overall problem can be represented as a multi-stage process. For this to be possible it is necessary that the final choices implied by the multi-stage process should be identical to those that arise when the overall allocation problem is solved in a single step. A necessary condition for this is that the consumer's preference ordering obeys certain fairly restrictive assumptions to be described later. However, these assumptions which have to be made about the class of utility functions representing this preference ordering lead to restrictions on demand equations which reduce the number of independent price and total expenditure responses. Thus methods (a) and (c) above of approaching the degrees of freedom problem are closely related. In fact the following should be intuitively clear.

In a multi-stage process the allocation of expenditure to any good or subgrouping of goods within a broader grouping is made using information concerning only total *group* expenditure and within-group prices. Hence, it must be possible to express demand for any good within a group simply as a function of total expenditure on the group to which it belongs and the prices

2.5 Multi-stage budgeting

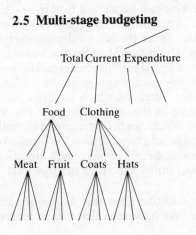

57

only of goods within that group. For example, in Fig. 2.5 it is clear that the price of hats can only influence the demand for meat via its influence on the overall expenditures on clothing and food.

We now consider in more detail the various ways of reducing the degrees-of-freedom problem, indicating in the process the interrelationships between the approaches. We begin with the most common assumptions that have been made about the form of the consumer's utility function.

Simplifying assumptions about consumer preferences

Additivity

Probably the assumption about consumer preferences that has been most widely used in empirical work is that of *additivity*. One method of defining additivity is to say that the consumer's (cardinal) utility function is such that the marginal utility of any good is independent of the quantities consumed of all other goods. This implies that the utility function is of the form

$$U = u_1(q_1) + u_2(q_2) + \cdots + u_n(q_n) \qquad [2.39]$$

so that the cross-partial derivatives U_{ij} are all zero. We have referred to this previously as the case of want independence. It is sometimes argued that such a property is acceptable provided that the 'goods' are defined to be sufficiently broad aggregates. For example, the marginal utility of one extra unit of 'food' is unlikely to be influenced by the number of units of 'clothing' consumed. However, such arguments presuppose that it is permissible to group commodities into such broad aggregates.

The Hessian matrix of the above utility function is diagonal as, hence, is its inverse which implies that $U^{ij} = 0$ for all $i \neq j$. Thus, from equation [2.34] we see that additivity implies that all specific cross-substitution effects are zero. The total cross-substitution effects, however, are not zero since the general substitution effects do not disappear – all commodities still compete in a general way for the consumer's expenditure.

The difficulty with the above definition of additivity is that the property is not invariant under non-linear monotonic transformations of the utility function. For example, the utility functions $U = \Sigma_i \log u_i(q_i)$ and $V = e^U = \Pi_i u_i(q_i)$ represent exactly the same preference ordering and hence will lead to exactly the same consumer choices for given total expenditure and prices. However, while the first of these functions is additive under the above definition, the second has $U_{ij} \neq 0$ and hence is non-additive. The notion of additivity, however, has been regarded as too attractive to be abandoned for this reason and may be reformulated as follows. A consumer's *preference ordering* is said to be additive if it can be represented by a class of utility functions which contains, as a subclass, utility functions which are additive in the sense described above. Thus, for example, the preference ordering which can be represented by both $U = \Sigma_i \log u_i(q_i)$ and $V = \Pi_i u_i(q_i)$ is said to be additive because the former of these utility functions is additive. It may well be asked why such attention should be given to any particular subclass of utility functions but this should become clearer as we proceed.

If a consumer's preference ordering is additive then this has important observable consequences for his behaviour. We have seen that if such preferences are represented by an additive utility function, the specific cross-substitution effects disappear and we have, from equation [2.34], for the total cross-substitution effect

$$k_{ij} = \frac{\partial q_i}{\partial p_j} + q_j \frac{\partial q_i}{\partial m} = -\left(\frac{\lambda}{\partial \lambda / \partial m}\right)\left(\frac{\partial q_i}{\partial m} \frac{\partial q_j}{\partial m}\right) = \mu\left(\frac{\partial q_i}{\partial m}\right)\left(\frac{\partial q_j}{\partial m}\right)$$

$$\text{all } i \neq j \quad [2.40]$$

where $\mu = -\lambda/(\partial \lambda / \partial m) > 0$ since $\lambda > 0$ and $\delta \lambda / \delta m < 0$.

Equation [2.40] indicates that when preferences are additive, cross-substitution effects are equal to a positive quantity (independent of i and j) times the product of the two income derivatives $\partial q_i / \partial m$ and $\partial q_j / \partial m$. As already stressed, the sizes of the specific and general substitution effects are not invariant under non-linear transformations of utility. However, both the quantities k_{ij} and the two income derivatives are observable quantities and hence invariant. Thus equation [2.40] will still hold for any utility function that can represent an additive preference ordering and hence it is implied by such an ordering. The quantity μ, however, cannot be unambiguously interpreted as being equal to $-\lambda/(\delta \lambda / \delta m)$ because neither λ nor $\delta \lambda / \delta m$ are themselves invariant.[12]

Equation [2.40] can be rewritten as

$$\frac{\partial q_i}{\partial p_j} = \left(\mu \frac{\partial q_j}{\partial m} - q_j\right)\left(\frac{\partial q_i}{\partial m}\right) = \theta \frac{\partial q_i}{\partial m} \quad \text{for all } i \neq j \quad [2.41]$$

where $\theta = \mu(\partial q_j / \partial m) - q_j$ is independent of i but dependent on j. *Thus additivity implies that if the price of any given good j changes, the cross-price responses of all other goods to this price change are proportional to their total expenditure responses.* The factor of proportionality, θ, however depends on the good whose price has changed.

Equations such as [2.41] imply that additivity involves a considerable reduction in the number of independent price and total expenditure responses and this is obviously helpful from the point of view of estimation. However, the full implications of additivity are in fact very restrictive indeed. Firstly, for example, there can be no inferior goods. This can be seen from the formula above equation [2.22], which implies that for an additive utility function

$$\frac{\partial q_i}{\partial m} = \frac{\partial \lambda}{\partial m} p_i U^{ii} > 0 \quad \text{for all } i$$

in the general case. Since the income derivatives are invariant, additive preferences must imply that they are all positive. Secondly, complementarity in the Hicksian sense is not possible under additivity. Since all income derivatives and μ are positive, equation [2.40] implies $k_{ij} > 0$ for all $i \neq j$ so that all cross-substitution effects are positive.

To rule out inferiority and Hicksian complementarity may alone appear too restrictive but, in addition, additivity implies that the number of remaining independent price and total expenditure responses is very few indeed. The aggregation restrictions imply that there are only $n - 1$ independent income derivatives anyway. Given these derivatives plus an estimate of μ, equation [2.41] determines all the cross-price derivatives for any given configuration of prices and total expenditure. Finally, the homogeneity restriction may be used to determine the own-price derivatives. That is, using equation [2.15A]

$$\frac{\partial q_i}{\partial p_i} p_i = -\sum_{j \neq i} \frac{\partial q_i}{\partial p_j} p_j - m \frac{\partial q_i}{\partial m}$$

$$= -\mu \frac{\partial q_i}{\partial m} \sum_{j \neq i} p_j \frac{\partial q_j}{\partial m} + \frac{\partial q_i}{\partial m} \sum_{j \neq i} p_j q_j - m \frac{\partial q_i}{\partial m} \qquad \text{(using [2.41])}$$

$$= -\mu \frac{\partial q_i}{\partial m} \left(1 - p_i \frac{\partial q_i}{\partial m}\right) - \frac{\partial q_i}{\partial m} p_i q_i$$

(using [2.13A] and $\Sigma p_j q_j = m$)

Hence

$$\frac{\partial q_i}{\partial p_i} = -\frac{\mu}{p_i} \frac{\partial q_i}{\partial m} + \frac{\partial q_i}{\partial m}\left(\mu \frac{\partial q_i}{\partial m} - q_i\right) \qquad i = 1, 2, 3, \ldots, n \qquad [2.42]$$

In practice this means that with knowledge of just n independent derivatives – the $n - 1$ income derivatives and any single price derivative – we can obtain μ from equation [2.41] and hence obtain all the remaining price derivatives using [2.41] and [2.42]. Additivity therefore implies that *there are only n independent responses in the model*. Provided one is prepared to accept additivity as a reasonable assumption, this is a considerable advantage in estimation. For example, it facilitates the estimation of price responses when, as with time series, there is little price variation in the data. However, estimates of price responses are then really made by assumption – the assumption of additivity – so that the reliability of such estimates is very much dependent on the appropriateness of the additivity assumption.

Deaton (1974b) draws attention to the severely restrictive nature of equation [2.42] in particular. By multiplying throughout by p_i/q_i we may express this equation in terms of elasticities:

$$\varepsilon_{ii} = -\frac{\mu}{m} \varepsilon_i - \varepsilon_i w_i \left(1 - \frac{\mu}{m} \varepsilon_i\right) \qquad [2.43]$$

where ε_{ii} and ε_i are the own-price and total expenditure elasticities of the ith good. Since all the budget shares, w_i, lie between zero and unity, if the number of goods n is large than each individual w_i will be small so that we will have $\varepsilon_{ii} \simeq -(\mu/m)\varepsilon_i$. That is the *own-price elasticities* are approximately proportional to the expenditure elasticities. Deaton refers to this as Pigou's law after a similar suggestion made by Pigou early in the century.

Strong separability

There are a number of useful ways in which the rather restrictive assumption of additivity can be relaxed. The aim is to increase the number of independent responses beyond the n implied by additivity, yet keep their number well below what would have to be estimated in the absence of any particular assumptions about the consumer's preference ordering. The most common is known as *strong separability* (or, alternatively, additive separability). This concept envisages a series of groupings of goods such that *the groups are want-independent*. That is the marginal utility of any good within a given group is independent of quantities consumed of goods outside that group. Obviously such groupings are, again, 'food', 'clothing', 'entertainment', etc. The concept implies a (cardinal) utility function of the form

$$U = u_1(\mathbf{q}_1) + u_2(\mathbf{q}_2) + u_3(\mathbf{q}_3) + \cdots + u_n(\mathbf{q}_n) \qquad [2.44]$$

where $\mathbf{q}_i$ now refers to the *vector* of commodities in the ith group. Equation [2.44] implies that the groups are want-independent since $U_{ij} = 0$ whenever good i and good j belong to different groups. The Hessian matrix U is 'block diagonal' and, hence, so is its inverse. We therefore have $U^{ij} = 0$ whenever i and j refer to different groups. Hence specific cross-substitution effects are zero for goods belonging to different groups, but not necessarily zero for goods within the same group.

Strong separability, like additivity, is a property that is not invariant under non-linear transformations of the utility function. However, like additivity, the concept can be reformulated. We can define a preference ordering as strongly separable provided the class of utility functions by which it may be represented contains, as a subclass, utility functions that have the property of strong separability. Again it may be objected that any subclass should not be given such special attention in defining a property of a preference ordering. However, the advantage of this approach, as we shall see, is that it enables the empirical investigator to make use of his *a priori* knowledge concerning the structure of consumer preferences. For example, it clearly makes more sense to include 'butter' in the group that includes 'bread' and 'margarine' than in the group that contains 'shirts'.

Like additivity, strong separability has important implications for the price and income responses in the consumer's demand equations. Specific cross-substitution effects are now zero only for goods in different groups so that equations [2.40] and [2.41] must be rewritten as

$$k_{ij} = \mu \, \frac{\partial q_i}{\partial m} \, \frac{\partial q_j}{\partial m}$$

for all i in any one group and all j in any other group $\qquad [2.45]$

and hence

$$\frac{\partial q_i}{\partial p_j} = \theta \, \frac{\partial q_i}{\partial m}$$

for all i in any one group and all j in any other group $\qquad [2.46]$

μ is again independent of i and j, and θ is again independent of i but dependent on j. Thus from [2.46] we see that strong separability implies that if the price of a given commodity in any one group changes, the price responses of all commodities *outside* that group are proportional to their income responses. However, the factor of proportionality, θ, again depends on the good whose price has changed. For goods *within* the same group, however, these relationships between cross-price and income derivatives no longer hold. This reflects the more limited restrictiveness of strong separability as compared with additivity.

We note at this point that our derivation of equations such as [2.40] and [2.45] is based on equation [2.34]. Since equation [2.34] is itself only derivable under the assumption of strictly convex preferences, it may appear that equations [2.40] and [2.45] are also dependent on this assumption. However, as we shall see shortly, equations [2.40] and [2.45] in fact hold whether preferences are convex or not.

Weak separability

A consumer's preferences are said to be 'weakly separable' when the goods he purchases can be divided into groups such that the consumer can rank all possible 'bundles' of goods within one group into a well-defined ordering which is independent of the quantities consumed of all goods outside the group. That is, within-group preferences are independent of purchases outside the group. A necessary and sufficient condition for *weak separability* is that preferences can be represented by a class of utility functions of the form

$$U = f[u_1(\mathbf{q}_1), u_2(\mathbf{q}_2), u_3(\mathbf{q}_3), \cdots u_n(\mathbf{q}_n)] \qquad [2.47]$$

where f is an increasing function of all its arguments. $\mathbf{q}_i$ again refers to the *vector* of commodities contained in group i and the $u_i(\mathbf{q}_i)$ are known as *subutility functions*. Utility functions of the form [2.47] imply that the marginal rate of substitution between any two goods in the same group is independent of quantities consumed outside the group. This reflects the 'preference independence' described above.

Notice that strong separability is the special case of weak separability where the subutility functions are simply added together. Notice also that the concept of weak separability was originally defined in terms of the consumer's preference ordering (marginal rates of substitution, unlike marginal utilities, are invariant under non-linear transformations of the utility function). We do not, therefore, face the difficulty of having to single out a particular subclass of utility functions as we have to do when redefining additivity or strong separability. Weak separability is an ordinal concept.

The importance of weak separability is that it is the necessary and sufficient condition for the *second stage* of the procedure of two-stage budgeting described at the beginning of this section. The quantities purchased of goods appearing in any one of the groups to which the subutility functions in [2.47] refer can always be expressed as functions of total *group* expenditure and within group prices alone. To see that weak separability implies such demand functions, consider the maximisation of equation [2.47]. This must involve the maximisation of each subutility function subject to the constraint on total expenditure on goods within that group. Otherwise, one of the $u_i(\mathbf{q}_i)$ could be increased (hence increasing U since f is an increasing function of each $u_i(\mathbf{q}_i)$), without violating the overall budget constraint. But maximisation of, for example $u_G(\mathbf{q}_G)$ subject to the constraint $\Sigma p_i q_i = m_G$, where the summation is over all i in group G and m_G is total expenditure on group G, leads to demand functions of the form

$$q_i = G_i(m_G, \mathbf{p}_G) \text{ for all } i \text{ in group } G \qquad [2.48]$$

where $\mathbf{p}_G$ represents a vector of the prices of goods in group G only.

Although more difficult to demonstrate it is also true that the existence of demand functions such as [2.48] implies weak separability, i.e. the existence of a subutility function $u_G(\mathbf{q}_G)$. Notice that, since strong separability is a special case of weak separability, it is also a sufficient condition for the existence of demand functions such as [2.48]. However, being a more restrictive assumption than weak separability, it is not a necessary condition.

The restricted nature of the arguments in [2.48] means that a change in total expenditure m, or a change in the price of any commodity j outside group G, only influences the demand for goods within group G via their effects on total group expenditure m_G. A further inspection of Fig. 2.5 should make this intuitively clear. Formally

$$\frac{\partial q_i}{\partial p_j} = \frac{\partial q_i}{\partial m_G}\frac{\partial m_G}{\partial p_j}$$

$$\text{for any } i \text{ in group } G \text{ and any } j \text{ in any other group } H \qquad [2.49]$$

and

$$\frac{\partial q_i}{\partial m} = \frac{\partial q_i}{\partial m_G}\frac{\partial m_G}{\partial m} \qquad \text{for any } i \text{ in group } G \qquad [2.50]$$

It follows from [2.49] and [2.50] that

$$\frac{\partial q_i/\partial p_j}{\partial q_i/\partial m} = \frac{\partial m_G/\partial p_j}{\partial m_G/\partial m}$$

or

$$\frac{\partial q_i}{\partial p_j} = \theta_G \frac{\partial q_i}{\partial m}$$

$$\text{for any } i \text{ in group } G \text{ and any } j \text{ in any other group } H \qquad [2.51]$$

where $\theta_G = (\partial m_G/\partial p_j)/(\partial m_G/\partial m)$ depends on *both* the group to which good i belongs *and* the good j whose price has changed. Thus when the price of any good j outside group G changes, the cross-price responses of all commodities within group G are proportional to their income responses. Notice that equation [2.51] is a generalisation of [2.46], which holds under strong separability. In the latter case the factor of proportionality θ was not dependent on the group to which the good whose responses we were considering belonged.

The equivalent generalisation of equation [2.45] can be obtained if we consider, under weak separability, the effect of price changes when utility is held constant. For any i in group G and any j in any other group H, we have

$$k_{ij} = \frac{\partial q_i}{\partial p_j}\bigg|_{U=\text{const}} = \frac{\partial q_i}{\partial m_G}\left(\frac{\partial m_G}{\partial p_j}\bigg|_{U=\text{const}}\right) \qquad [2.52]$$

$$k_{ji} = \frac{\partial q_j}{\partial p_i}\bigg|_{U=\text{const}} = \frac{\partial q_j}{\partial m_H}\left(\frac{\partial m_H}{\partial p_i}\bigg|_{U=\text{const}}\right) \qquad [2.53]$$

where m_H is total expenditure on group H. However, symmetry implies $k_{ij} = k_{ji}$ so we have

$$\frac{\partial q_i}{\partial m_G}\left(\frac{\partial m_G}{\partial p_j}\bigg|_{U=\text{const}}\right) = \frac{\partial q_j}{\partial m_H}\left(\frac{\partial m_H}{\partial p_i}\bigg|_{U=\text{const}}\right) \qquad [2.54]$$

Hence

$$\frac{\partial m_G}{\partial p_j}\bigg|_{U=\text{const}} = \lambda_{GH}\frac{\partial q_j}{\partial m_H} \qquad [2.55]$$

where

$$\lambda_{GH} = \left(\frac{\partial m_H}{\partial p_i}\bigg|_{U=\text{const}}\right)\bigg/\frac{\partial q_i}{\partial m_G} = \left(\frac{\partial m_G}{\partial p_j}\bigg|_{U=\text{const}}\right)\bigg/\frac{\partial q_j}{\partial m_H} \qquad [2.56]$$

Clearly, λ_{GH} in [2.55] depends both on the group to which good i belongs and on the group to which good j belongs. In addition, however, since the first expression for λ_{GH} in [2.56] is independent of j, and the second expression is independent of i, we can see that λ_{GH} must be the same for all i in group G and all j in group H. Hence, substituting [2.55] into [2.52] we have

$$k_{ij} = \lambda_{GH} \frac{\partial q_i}{\partial m_G} \frac{\partial q_j}{\partial m_H}$$

for all i in group G and all j in group H [2.57]

or, using [2.50] and its equivalent for group H,

$$k_{ij} = \mu_{GH} \frac{\partial q_i}{\partial m} \frac{\partial q_j}{\partial m}$$

for all i in group G and all j in group H [2.58]

where

$$\mu_{GH} = \lambda_{GH} \Big/ \left(\frac{\partial m_G}{\partial m} \frac{\partial m_H}{\partial m} \right).$$

Thus the cross-substitution effects are again proportional to the product of the total expenditure derivatives, but, unlike in equation [2.45] for the case of strong separability, the factor of proportionality depends on *both* the groups to which goods i and j belong. Vary either of these groups and the factor of proportionality changes. Under strong separability, since the utility function [2.47] is additive, new groups can be arbitrarily formed by combining original groups and this rules out the possibility that the proportionality factor should be dependent on the groups involved. Hence given strong separability, equation [2.58] reduces to equation [2.45]. Also, of course, under additivity, since each group now contains only one good, equation [2.58] reduces to equation [2.40].

Notice that the derivation of equation [2.58] above does not require the assumption of strictly convex preferences. Since equations [2.40] and [2.45] are derivable from the more general equation [2.58], we see that these equations are also independent of the convex preferences assumption, although we required this assumption for our original derivation.

From equation [2.58] we see that weak separability implies that, while substitution between goods within the same group is in no way restricted, substitution between goods in different groups must conform to group norms as represented by the μ_{GH}, although this conformity is modified by the total expenditure derivatives. This is so because, as we have seen, the price of a commodity in group H (e.g. 'food') can only influence demand for a commodity in group G (e.g. 'clothing') via its effect on total group G expenditure. That is, the intergroup price responses must follow the same 'lines of communication'. Further examination of Fig. 2.5 should make this self-evident.

We have already noted that strong separability enables us to utilise *a priori* notions about the structure of consumer preferences, grouping together goods which are closely linked in the yielding of 'utility'. Weak separability also enables us to do this but also has the advantage of being more easily definable in terms which are invariant under non-linear transformations of the utility function.

Aggregation over commodities

Provided the assumption of separability (weak or strong) proves acceptable, the problem of estimating demand systems clearly becomes more tractable. The number of independent price and income responses is considerably reduced and we can if we wish concentrate on subproblems within the consumer's overall allocation problem. For example, we can focus attention simply on the allocation of total *current* expenditure if preferences are 'intertemporally separable'.

The typical consumer, however, purchases a vast number of goods and, even if we can assume separability, the number of remaining price and total expenditure responses is still too large for them to be individually estimated. Clearly we need to be able to aggregate over the separable groups and form the composite commodities mentioned at the beginning of this subsection. Moreover, since available data series invariably refer to aggregates of commodities, this is a further reason for working, if possible, in such terms.

Suppose the consumer's allocation problem can be represented by a multi-stage process, the final stages of which are similar to those illustrated in Fig. 2.5. For estimation to be feasible with the limited time-spans of data likely to be available, we must either concentrate on the subproblem of allocating total current expenditure between the broad groups, 'food', 'clothing', etc., or on a subproblem involving the allocation of some broad group expenditure between various subgroups within that broad group. An example of the second type of problem might be the allocation of total food expenditure between 'meat', 'fruit', etc. In the first case we need to be able to form composite commodities out of the broad groups, while in the second case we need to be able to form them out of the subgroups such as 'meat' or 'fruit'. In either case, such composite commodities must have a 'quantity' measure and a 'price' measure such that their product equals total group expenditure. Moreover, these measures must satisfy the following property. If a consumer were to allocate between the composite commodities simply on the basis of the composite commodity 'prices', then the expenditures on the composite commodities that result must be the same as would occur if the allocation problems had been solved using the prices of all the individual goods that make up the composite commodities.

The first set of conditions under which groups of commodities can be treated in the same manner as individual goods was derived by Hicks (1956). Suppose relative prices within a group remain constant, i.e. $p_i = \gamma p_i^0$ where the p_i^0 are base year prices and γ, although varying over time, is the same for all i within the group. It is then not difficult to show that the group can be treated as a single commodity, satisfying the conditions of the previous paragraph. The 'price' of the commodity group is equal to γ and the 'quantity' equal to $\Sigma\, p_i^0 q_i$ – the weighted average of quantities of the individual goods in the group with weights equal to the base year prices.

In practice the empirical influence of the Hicks result is limited since relative prices within groups are likely to change over anything but the shortest interval of time. This fact has led to attempts to determine what types of consumer preference ordering represent necessary and sufficient conditions not merely for the second but also the first stage of two-stage budgeting – that is, the aggregation over commodity groups. Gorman (1959) provided two sets of conditions, both rather restrictive and one involving strong separability. Unfortunately it turns out that weak separability while, as we have seen, sufficient for the second stage, *is not a sufficient condition for the first stage of two-stage budgeting*. The reason for this is that while 'price' and 'quantity' measures can be derived from the broad groups under weak separability, the price measure is a function of the maximum value of the relevant subutility function. This in turn is dependent on the prices of the individual goods in the group. However, in practice it may be the case that the empirical relationship between these group price measures and utility is sufficiently weak for them to be well approximated by the Laspeyres and Paasche price indices that are usually available.

It is clear from the above that if we are to make use of the most attractive of the assumptions we have considered about consumer preferences, i.e. weak separability, then we must resort to approximations. Only then can we make use of the notion of composite commodities in a reasonably satisfactory theoretical manner. However, it is quite possible that the consumer himself may resort to such approximations. Suppose preferences are weakly separable but 'perfect' multi-stage budgeting is not possible; that is, it does not lead to purchases of individual goods identical to those that would occur when the allocation problem is solved in one step. Despite this, a consumer may well resort to some kind of 'imperfect' multi-stage budgeting rather than face the impossibly complex problem of simultaneously determining the optimal purchases of the multitude of goods available to him. That is, he may abandon precise utility maximisation and adopt the 'hierarchical' approach, using as broad group prices and quantity measures any roughly appropriate indices that are available.

Once it has been (unavoidably) decided, with whatever justification, to aggregate over commodity groups, one possible choice that has to be made (or tested for) is whether to treat the groups formed as weakly separable or strongly separable. If we assume strong separability, then we are really back in the position of accepting additivity, although the restrictive implications of this assumption now apply only to the commodity aggregates and no longer to individual goods. For example, commodity groups cannot be inferior and complementarity between groups is ruled out. If merely weak separability between groups is assumed then of course these restrictions are not implied.

Aggregation over consumers

The fact that available data usually refer to the combined expenditures of many households raises two questions. The first we have already discussed in the context of the single-equation approach – that of whether, given a set of 'micro-demand equations' for individual consumers, there exists a 'macro-demand equation' of exactly the same functional form as the micro-functions. The second is that of whether, given the existence of such macro-functions, they can be expected to satisfy restrictions derived from a theory that relates to a single consumer. That is, even if the micro-functions satisfy these restrictions, will such properties 'carry over' to the macro-function? Only if the answer to this second question is 'yes' is it obviously legitimate to impose the general theoretical restrictions on aggregate demand equations or to use aggregate data to test the validity of such restrictions.

In the full system approach, we have already noted that neither linear demand systems such as [2.28] or [2.29] nor log–linear systems such as [2.30] are capable of completely satisfying all the general restrictions at the micro-level. Hence they are obviously not capable of doing so at the macro-level. In fact, the conditions under which the perfect aggregation of a system of demand equations is possible are the same as those derived for the single demand equation. All households must have demand equations which are linear functions of total expenditure and the marginal propensity to spend on any good must be the same for all households. That is, the hth household's demand for the ith good must be of the form

$$q_i^h = a_{0i}^h(\mathbf{p}) + a_{1i}(\mathbf{p})m^h \qquad [2.59]$$

where $\mathbf{p}$ is the vector of all prices and, while the functions a_{0i}^h may vary across households, the function a_{1i} *may not*. Only if the micro-demand equations are of this form can we aggregate and obtain a macro-equation of identical functional form, that is

$$\bar{q}_i = a_{0i}(\mathbf{p}) + a_{1i}(\mathbf{p})\bar{m} \qquad [2.60]$$

where $\bar{q}_i$ and $\bar{m}$ are the arithmetic means of individual demands and total expenditures. The aggregate a_{0i} function is the arithmetic mean of the a_{0i}^h functions.

As far as the general theoretical restrictions are concerned, it turns out that provided they are satisfied by the micro-equations [2.59] they will automatically be satisfied by the macro-equations [2.60]. Hence no further conditions are necessary to ensure a theoretically satisfactory system of macro-demand equations. To see this, suppose all households have cost functions of the form

$$m_h = b_1^h(\mathbf{p}) + U^h b_2(\mathbf{p}) \qquad [2.61]$$

where U^h is the utility of the hth household and the function $b_1^h(\mathbf{p})$ varies from household to household but the function $b_2(\mathbf{p})$ does not. To be consistent with utility maximisation/cost minimisation, $b_1^h(\mathbf{p})$ and $b_2(\mathbf{p})$ must be such as to ensure that [2.61] possesses all the properties of cost functions listed earlier. For example, $b_1^h(\mathbf{p})$ and $b_2(\mathbf{p})$ must both be concave in any one price for given values of the other prices.

It is left to the reader to demonstrate that the cost function [2.61] implies Marshallian demand functions of the form [2.59] which are linear in total expenditure and for which $a_{1i}(\mathbf{p})$ is the same for all households. With greater difficulty it can also be shown that [2.61] is the *only* cost function that leads to demand functions of the form [2.59]. That is, if we assume demand functions of this form, cost functions of the form [2.61] are necessarily implied. Moreover, [2.61] can be aggregated without difficulty, since summing over all h and dividing by the total number of households yields

$$\bar{m} = b_1(\mathbf{p}) + \bar{U}b_2(\mathbf{p}) \qquad [2.62]$$

where $\bar{m}$ is mean expenditure and $\bar{U}$ is mean utility. $b_1(\mathbf{p})$ is the mean of the $b_1^h(\mathbf{p})$'s. The cost function [2.62] is clearly that underlying the demand equations [2.60]. But since [2.61] possesses all the properties necessary to be a consumer cost function so must [2.62]. Hence [2.62] is consistent with utility maximisation/cost minimisation and it follows that the demand equations [2.60] must satisfy all the general restrictions implied by this.

The reader should note at this point that the utility maximisation referred to and the preferences underlying [2.62] are those of some imaginary 'representative consumer' who happens to possess the mean total expenditure $\bar{m}$.[13] All we are saying is that the aggregate equations [2.60] can be regarded *as if* they result from the choices of such a representative consumer. This is all we need claim for the aggregate equations [2.60] to satisfy the restrictions of theory.

The aggregation of non-linear Engel curves
The individual household demand equations [2.59] can, then, be satisfactorily aggregated. However, equations [2.59] are themselves very restrictive, implying that all Engel curves are *linear* and that the Engel curves of different households all have the same slope. As we have already observed in Section 1.5, most empirical studies of Engel curves have strongly suggested that they are non-linear. However, Muellbauer (1975) and (1976) in fact demonstrated that it is possible to aggregate *non-linear* Engel curves, provided that aggregate demands are expressed as functions of 'representative expenditure' rather than mean expenditure.

Muellbauer is able to show that, provided the individual household cost functions are of a certain form, then it is possible to aggregate budget share equations for individual households into an aggregate equation which can be regarded as derived from the cost function of some 'representative' utility maximising household. This representative household is simply an imaginary household possessed of 'representative expenditure' (to be defined shortly). Since they are derivable from the cost function of such a household, the aggregate budget share equations must satisfy the restrictions implied by consumer theory.

In the Muellbauer framework, aggregate budget shares are dependent on all prices and representative expenditure (i.e. the expenditure of the representative household) which is itself a function of all prices and the distribution of individual household expenditures. An interesting and useful special case is when representative expenditure is independent of prices and depends only on the distribution of household expenditures. If satisfactory aggregation is to be possible for this case, the Muellbauer analysis indicates that the individual cost functions have to take the form

$$m^h = k^h[b_1(\mathbf{p})^\alpha(1 - U^h) + b_2(\mathbf{p})^\alpha U^h]^{1/\alpha} \qquad [2.63]$$

where α and k^h are parameters, while the cost function of the representative household is

$$m_0 = [b_1(\mathbf{p})^\alpha(1 - U_0) + b_2(\mathbf{p})^\alpha U_0]^{1/\alpha} \qquad [2.64]$$

The special case represented by equations [2.63] and [2.64] is known as that of *price independent generalised linearity* (PIGL). When α tends to zero, it can be shown that these cost functions approach

$$\log m^h = \log k^h + (1 - U^h) \log b_1(\mathbf{p}) + U^h \log b_2(\mathbf{p}) \qquad [2.63A]$$

for the individual household and

$$\log m^0 = (1 - U_0) \log b_1(\mathbf{p}) + U_0 \log b_2(\mathbf{p}) \qquad [2.64A]$$

for the representative household. This particularly convenient and useful logarithmic form is, for obvious reasons, known as the PIGLOG case.

Using Shephard's lemma, we can derive the individual and representative budget share equations for the PIGLOG case from [2.63A] and [2.64A]. For the individual household we obtain

$$w_i^h = a_{0i} + a_{1i} \log\left(\frac{m^h}{k^h}\right) \qquad i = 1, 2, 3, \ldots, n \qquad [2.65]$$

and for the representative household

$$\bar{w}_i = a_{0i} + a_{1i} \log m_0 \qquad i = 1, 2, 3, \ldots, n \qquad [2.66]$$

$\bar{w}_i$ is the aggregate budget share for the ith good, m_0 is representative expenditure and a_{0i} and a_{1i} are functions of prices only.

Notice that the Engel curves implied by [2.65] are non-linear.[14] For example, if $k^h = 1$ for all households, the Engel curves take the form

$$p_i q_i^h = a_{0i} m^h + a_{1i} m^h \log m^h \qquad [2.65A]$$

Engel curves of the form [2.65A] have a long history in empirical work, dating as far back as Working (1943) and are well known for providing very close fits to a wide range of cross-sectional data.

We can derive an expression for representative expenditure in the PIGLOG case by using the fact that the equations [2.65] can be aggregated to form [2.66]. Notice that

$$\bar{w}_i = \frac{\Sigma_h \, p_i q_i^h}{\Sigma_h \, m^h} = \sum_h \frac{m^h}{\Sigma_h \, m^h} \cdot w_i^h$$

That is, the aggregate budget share for good i is a weighted average of household budget shares, with weights equal to the share of each household in total expenditure for the good. Hence, using [2.65] and [2.66]

$$a_{0i} + a_{1i} \log m_0 = \sum_h \frac{m^h}{\Sigma_h \, m^h} \left[a_{0i} + a_{1i} \log\left(\frac{m^h}{k^h}\right) \right]$$

$$= a_{0i} + a_{1i} \left[\frac{\Sigma \, m^h \log \, (m^h/k^h)}{\Sigma \, m^h} \right]$$

Thus representative expenditure in the PIGLOG case is given by

$$\log m_0 = \frac{\Sigma \, m^h \log \, (m^h/k^h)}{\Sigma \, m^h} \qquad [2.67]$$

Let us summarise the argument so far. Provided each household has the cost function [2.63A] and hence budget share equations [2.65], it is possible to aggregate the budget share equation for any good into an equation, given by [2.66]. This equation can be regarded *as if* it were the budget share equation of a representative utility maximising household possessing the cost function [2.64A]. Representative expenditure in this cost function is given by equation [2.67]. Since the cost function [2.64A] is that of a utility maximising consumer, the aggregate budget share equations arising from it can be expected to obey all the general theoretical restrictions.

Notice that, since we can write [2.67] as

$$m_0 = \prod_h \left(\frac{m^h}{k^h}\right)^{m^h/\Sigma m^h}$$

representative expenditure m_0 is homogeneous of degree unity in the individual m^h's. For example, if all the individual m^h's double, then representative expenditure doubles, and in general equiproportionate changes in the m^h's lead to the same equiproportionate change in m_0. Moreover, a doubling in all m^h's also leads to a doubling in their arithmetic mean, $\bar{m}$, and in general equiproportionate changes in all m^h's lead to the same equiproportionate change in $\bar{m}$. Thus, provided the m^h's always change equiproportionately, i.e. *provided the distribution of total expenditures remains unchanged*, there will exist a proportionate relationship between representative expenditure and mean expenditure. Hence we can define an aggregate parameter k such that $\bar{m} = km_0$ and rewrite the aggregate budget share equations [2.66] as

$$\bar{w}_i = a_{0i} + a_{1i} \log\left(\frac{\bar{m}}{k}\right) \qquad [2.68]$$

Equation [2.68] is clearly analogous to the individual budget share equations [2.65].

It is now time to give an interpretation to the k_h parameters in equations [2.65] and the k parameter in equation [2.68]. Since k^h varies over households, it can be regarded as being determined by household size and composition. Notice that the Engel curves implied by [2.65] can be written as

$$\frac{p_i q_i^h}{k^h} = a_{0i}\left(\frac{m^h}{k^h}\right) + a_{1i}\left(\frac{m^h}{k^h}\right) \log\left(\frac{m^h}{k^h}\right) \qquad [2.69]$$

Thus if k^h is defined, crudely, as the number of persons in household h, then not only is [2.69] non-linear, but it expresses *per capita* expenditure on good i as a function of *per capita* total expenditure.

We can, however, give the k^h's a more sophisticated role than that of a simple head count. k^h can be interpreted as the index, reflecting the size, composition and other household attributes, that is required to deflate total expenditure m^h, if it is to be brought to a 'needs corrected' per capita level. As such, k^h would also reflect any economies of scale in household size. k^h is therefore exactly the same as the household size measured in terms of some equivalent adult scale that we discussed in Section 1.5.

The aggregate parameter, k, in [2.68] obviously measures the extent to which the representative expenditure differs from mean expenditure. This will normally depend both on the extent to which household tastes, as reflected by the k^h's, vary across households and on the dispersion in individual household expenditures. If all households had identical tastes (i.e. $k^h = 1$ for all h), k would simply be an index of the equality of the distribution of household m^h's. It would take its minimum value when all household total expenditures were identical. k will remain constant over time provided the distribution of household tastes remains unchanged and provided the only changes in household total expenditures are equiproportionate changes.

The reader will appreciate that the problem of aggregating over non-linear Engel curves is a complex one. It is, perhaps, not surprising that many investigators have preferred to ignore it, relying instead on the Hicksian argument outlined at the end of Section 1.2. However, Muellbauer's approach is beginning to make an impact on empirical studies and we shall refer to it again in Section 2.6 below.

2.6 Early complete system models of demand

Early workers in the field tended to adopt one of two possible approaches to the estimation of systems of demand equations. One approach was to specify a particular form for the utility function and derive the functional form of the demand equations from this utility function. Such a method guaranteed that the demand equations obtained would satisfy all the general restrictions implied by consumer theory and that there would be a corresponding reduction in the number of independent parameters that had to be estimated. The disadvantages of this approach are, firstly, that it cannot be used to *test* whether the restrictions of theory are satisfied by the data and, secondly, that there will invariably be some loss of generality resulting from whatever precise form is adopted for the utility function.

An alternative approach was to abandon any specific form for the utility function and to *start* with a set of demand equations which did not necessarily satisfy the restrictions of theory but were capable of doing so. Attempts were then made to test whether the data satisfied the theoretical restrictions by estimating the equations with and without the restrictions imposed. If the restrictions appeared to be confirmed they could then be accepted as constraints on the estimating procedure and used to obtain more precise estimates of the remaining independent parameters. The disadvantages of this second approach are, firstly, that since we begin the estimation procedure with no restrictions imposed we are faced with the problem of estimating the full quota of $n(n + 1)$ price and total expenditure responses. Limitations in sample size then inevitably mean that n has to be kept relatively small, i.e. the method can be used only for a relatively small number of commodity groups. Secondly, while this procedure may appear to circumvent the need to specify the precise form of the utility function there are problems. There is an ever-present danger that in specifying a particular functional form for the demand equations we are, without realising it, imposing restrictions (maybe totally implausible ones) on the type of utility function underlying the demand equations we have specified. We shall return to this problem shortly.

We begin this section by considering the two demand systems which, until a few years ago, were the most popular from the empirical point of view. These are the *linear expenditure system* (LES), which typifies the first of the two approaches outlined above, and the *Rotterdam model*, which is the best-known example of the second approach.

The linear expenditure system

This system was first extensively utilised by Stone (1954b), and has a precisely specified underlying utility function of the form

$$U = \sum_i \beta_i \log (q_i - \gamma_i) \qquad [2.70]$$

where the β_i and γ_i are parameters and we require that $q_i > \gamma_i$ in order that the logarithms be defined. We may divide this utility function by the sum of the β_i's without affecting the resultant demand equations since this merely involves applying a monotonic transformation to [2.70]. This is equivalent to 'normalising' these parameters or imposing the restriction that $\Sigma\,\beta_i = 1$. Also since $\partial U/\partial q_i = \beta_i/(q_i - \gamma_i) > 0$ we have that $\beta_i > 0$ which, together with the normalising condition, implies that $0 < \beta_i < 1$ for all i.

The maximisation of [2.70] subject to the usual budget constraint $\Sigma\,p_i q_i = m$ leads to demand equations of the form

$$q_i = \gamma_i + \frac{\beta_i}{p_i}\left(m - \sum_j p_j\gamma_j\right) \qquad i = 1, 2, 3, \ldots, n \qquad [2.71\text{A}]$$

or

$$p_i q_i = p_i\gamma_i + \beta_i\left(m - \sum_j p_j\gamma_j\right) \qquad i = 1, 2, 3, \ldots, n \qquad [2.71\text{B}]$$

Equations [2.71B] constitute the so-called *linear expenditure system*. Its great advantage is its linearity. Equation [2.71A] expresses the q_i as linear functions of m/p_i and of relative prices which is very convenient for estimation purposes. In fact it can be shown that [2.71A] is the only form of linear demand equation which satisfies all the theoretical restrictions.[15]

An attractive way of interpreting equation [2.71B] is to regard expenditure on good i, $p_i q_i$, as divided into two parts. Firstly, $p_i\gamma_i$ can be interpreted as the minimum subsistence level expenditure on good i, so that γ_i represents the subsistence level of q_i. This means that, of total expenditure m, a portion $\Sigma\,p_i\gamma_i$ is committed to necessary subsistence purchases. The remainder, $m - \Sigma\,p_j\gamma_j$, may be called 'supernumerary expenditure' and is allocated in constant proportions between all goods so that the second part of $p_i q_i$ consists of a constant proportion β_i of supernumary expenditure. Notice, however, that this interpretation implies the additional restriction that each γ_i be greater than zero.

While the simplicity of the LES is attractive it has obvious limitations. The underlying preference ordering is additive as an examination of its representation in equation [2.70] clearly indicates. We know that this rules out inferior goods and implies that all goods must be Hicksian substitutes. We have also seen that a further consequence of additivity is that cross-price derivatives are proportional to expenditure derivatives. Partially differentiating [2.71A] with respect to p_j and m yields

$$\frac{\partial q_i}{\partial p_j} = -\frac{\beta_i\,\gamma_j}{p_i} \quad \text{and} \quad \frac{\partial q_i}{\partial m} = \frac{\beta_i}{p_i}$$

so that in the present context equation [2.41] becomes

$$\frac{\partial q_i}{\partial p_j} = -\gamma_j\frac{\partial q_i}{\partial m} \qquad \text{for all } i \neq j \qquad [2.72]$$

or, alternatively,

$$\frac{\partial q_i/\partial p_j}{\partial q_k/\partial p_j} = \frac{\partial q_i/\partial m}{\partial q_k/\partial m} \quad \text{for any } i \text{ and } k \neq j \qquad [2.73]$$

This has important empirical implications when we are dealing with time series data for which, typically, variations in real total expenditure are much greater than variations in relative prices. When estimating either of equations [2.71A] or [2.71B] from such data, typically strong trends in q_i and m/p_i (a measure of real expenditure) lead to a high correlation between these variables. The β_i coefficients, and hence the income derivatives, therefore tend to be very well determined. However, lack of variation in relative prices, the p_j/p_i, means that the γ_j coefficients, and hence the price derivatives, will generally be much less precisely determined. The danger then is that the structure or *relative* size of the responses of the various goods to any given price change will, via equation [2.73], be determined simply by the relative size of the well-determined income responses. Given the well-determined income derivatives, the only role for any variation in relative prices in the data is, via equation [2.72], merely to determine, albeit imprecisely, the absolute size of the price derivatives. In the words of Brown and Deaton (1972): 'the linear expenditure system, like other additive models, will impose a structure on estimated price effects largely independently of the structure of actual price effects'.

Since its first extensive use by Stone, the LES, despite its drawbacks, has proved a most popular method of estimating expenditure and price responses that may then be used for forecasting purposes. Its attractiveness lies not only in its being a linear system satisfying all the requirements of theory but in the relatively few number of parameters that have to be estimated. Altogether there are only $2n$ parameters in the n-equation LES and since $\Sigma \beta_i = 1$, the number of independent parameters is $2n - 1$. This compares with, for example, the $\frac{1}{2}n(n + 1) - 1$ independent parameters of equation [2.33] which have to be estimated when merely the general theoretical restrictions are imposed. The reduction is, of course, the result of employing an additive utility function which places additional restrictions on the form of the demand equations. This reduction in the number of independent parameters, and the consequent increase in degrees of freedom implied, means that a far larger number of commodity classifications can be handled then with models which satisfy the general restrictions only. Unfortunately, the finer the classification of commodities adopted, the less realistic is the assumption of additivity likely to be.

Linear expenditure systems have been estimated for a wide variety of time periods and countries. In most cases investigators concentrated on the allocation of total current expenditure between various commodity groupings. Little but token attention was paid to problems of aggregation. Data were usually simply expressed in per capita form and it was implicitly assumed that the commodity groups formed could be treated as single 'goods'. Stone's original work used UK data for 1920–38, but he and his colleagues (1964) continued to use the system, projecting demand patterns up until 1970 using data since the beginning of the century. Other notable studies included those of Pollack and Wales (1969) using post-war US data, Parks (1969) with Swedish data and Yoshihara (1969) using Japanese data. There were also comparative studies involving different countries beginning with that of Goldberger and Gamaletsos (1970) who examined expenditure patterns for thirteen OECD countries. Later, Deaton (1975) estimated an LES for the UK involving 37 commodity groupings. Lluch et al. (1977) made wide use of the so-called extended linear expenditure system, in which total current expenditure is made endogenous and attention is focused on the allocation of total current *income* between savings and the various forms of current expenditure.

In the great majority of cases investigators seem to have regarded their results as reasonable. In most studies, the β_i's turn out to be positive and this is also true of the γ coefficients, suggesting that their interpretation as subsistence quantities is not unreasonable.

The Deaton (1975) study mentioned above was notable for the large number of commodity groupings used: 37 in all. Durable goods were excluded so that m is defined as total expenditure on non-durables. The normal LES was generalised slightly to allow the β_i to vary over time as a reflection of taste changes, so the form of equations estimated was in fact

$$p_i q_i = p_i \gamma_i + (\beta_i^0 + \beta_i^1 t)\left(m - \sum_j p_j \gamma_j\right) \qquad [2.74]$$

where t is a time trend, taking the value zero in 1963. Per-capita British data were used for 1954–70 and a maximum likelihood method of estimation employed. The 'fits' of all the equations were very close – in 22 cases out of the 37, R^2 exceeds 0.99 and in only 5 was it less than 0.95. However, these high coefficients of multiple determination were partly the result of common upward trend in all expenditure variables. Plots of actual against predicted *quantities* suggested that while this LES is good at following trend movements in demand it is not so successful in tracking cyclical fluctuations about such trends.

Income elasticities of demand are not constants in the LES but can be calculated for any given year. Deaton in fact estimated their 1963 values, when $\beta_i = \beta_i^0$ and hence income elasticities are given by $\varepsilon_i = \beta_i^0/w_i$. The ranking of the ε_i obtained this way appeared intuitively reasonable with foodstuffs, for example, having low elasticities but with such obvious luxuries as recreational goods, cosmetics, etc., having much higher ones.

The interpretation of the own-price elasticities obtained is complicated by 'Pigou's law' which was outlined below equation [2.43]. A comparison of equations [2.41] and [2.72] indicates that for the LES $\mu(\partial q_j/\partial m) - q_j = -\gamma_j$. Hence, once the γ_j have been estimated, the own-price elasticities, ε_{ii}, for any given year can be derived from the total expenditure elasticities using equation [2.43]. Since the number of commodity groupings is large, each individual budget share w_i is small. So 'Pigou's law' is likely to hold with the own-price elasticities proportional to the total expenditure elasticities. In fact, Deaton's examination of the 1963 values for those estimated elasticities revealed that the ratio $\varepsilon_i/\varepsilon_{ii}$ was virtually a constant of about -0.21 to -0.23. The danger now is that this remarkably close relationship is not a property of the data but purely a consequence of the model used. To check against this possibility Deaton also estimated log–linear demand equations of the form

$$\log q_i = \alpha_i + (\varepsilon_i^0 + \varepsilon_i^1 t) \log\left(\frac{m}{\pi}\right) + (\varepsilon_{ii}^0 + \varepsilon_{ii}^1 t) \log\left(\frac{p_i}{\pi}\right) \qquad [2.75]$$

for all 37 commodity groupings. π is a general index of prices. For the 1963 own-price and total expenditure elasticities, no close relationship this time emerged. In fact, for these estimates, the simple coefficient of correlation between ε_i and ε_{ii} was as low as 0.0088. Thus it appears that, while the considerable variation in total expenditure during the sample period permitted fairly precise estimates of total expenditure elasticities to be obtained, the lack of price information in the data means that the model used was able to impose its own pattern on the own-price elasticities.

The Rotterdam model

This model typifies the second approach to demand system estimation outlined at the beginning of this section – the attempt to find a set of demand equations capable of, but not necessarily satisfying, all the general theoretical restrictions. It proved the most popular early vehicle for attempting to test the validity of these restrictions.

The Rotterdam model was first developed by Theil (1965) and Barten (1966) and is based on equation [2.32] with dependent variables of the form w_i d-log q_i, i.e. the 'endogenous' change in budget shares. It is an example of a differential demand system – that is, it deals with the changes in, rather than the levels of, demand. *As written in equation [2.32] such a demand system is completely general in the sense that it can be derived from any underlying utility function.* However, if [2.32] is to be estimated, then the differentials have to be approximated by first differences (e.g. d log q_i has to be replaced by log q_{it} − log q_{it-1}) and the μ_i and the π_{ij} have to be regarded as constants or parameters. We noted earlier that provided the μ_i and the π_{ij} are treated in this way then the system has the great advantage that all the general theoretical restrictions remain unchanged for all values of total expenditure and prices and hence *for every observation in a sample.* They are also (apart from the negativity restriction) of very simple form. The Rotterdam model, then, appeared to be a convenient and powerful vehicle for the testing of consumer theory.

Typically a maximum likelihood approach was used in estimation. Values of the maximised likelihood obtained when the system was estimated without restrictions could then be compared with the likelihood obtained when the restrictions were imposed one by one. If the imposition of any restriction resulted in a fall in the likelihood value, greater than could be expected to occur by chance when the restriction is valid, then the data were said to have rejected the restriction. It should be noted at this point that it is not possible to 'test' the aggregation restrictions [2.13C] and [2.14C] when the data 'add up' as they normally do in the sense that the sum of expenditure on individual goods equals the total expenditure variable, m. Since the aggregation restrictions are merely properties of the budget constraint, estimates of equations such as [2.32] will then automatically satisfy the aggregation restriction.

As already observed, a disadvantage of the present approach is that unrestricted estimation involves large numbers of independent parameters. This means that problems of sample size and degrees of freedom generally restrict the number of commodity groups that can be accommodated within the model. The largest Rotterdam model ever estimated was probably that of Barten (1969) who included 16 equations in his model.

Barten, using Dutch data for 1921–63, estimated his system firstly in the absence of any restrictions (apart from aggregation), then with homogeneity (equation [2.15C]) imposed, and finally with symmetry (equation [2.25C]) imposed. In each case intercept terms were added to the basic Rotterdam-type equation to allow for changes in taste. When homogeneity was imposed there was a large fall in the likelihood value obtained – far larger than could be expected by chance. Barten's data therefore did not appear to support the theoretical proposition that equiproportionate changes in prices and total expenditure should leave demands unchanged. The symmetry restrictions were similarly rejected but as Deaton (1972) pointed out, if homogeneity is taken as given, it may be that the *additional* restriction of symmetry need not be rejected. Deaton (1974a) in fact estimated a nine-equation Rotterdam model, using similar procedures to Barten but with UK data for 1900–70. He obtained similar results to Barten. Intercept terms were significant, homogeneity was rejected by the data and so was symmetry. However, when symmetry (which implies homogeneity if the aggregation restrictions are necessarily met) was imposed the likelihood value was not significantly lower than when homogeneity alone was imposed. Hence, as seemed possible from Barten's study, it appeared to be only the homogeneity aspects of symmetry that are rejected by actual data. Other investigators obtained essentially similar results.[16]

A further interesting aspect of the Deaton study is that when the restrictions on the Rotterdam system implied by 'additivity' were imposed, these restrictions were also rejected by the data. Since Deaton was dealing with commodity groups rather than individual goods this result, as far as it goes, suggests that consumer preferences are not strongly separable in the sense defined in the previous section. At least they are not strongly separable over the commodity groups used in the Deaton study. This, however, is perhaps not too surprising since there are likely to be substitution effects between even quite broad commodity groups which are too 'specific' to be permitted under any form of 'want-independence'.

The fact that Rotterdam-type studies appeared invariably to result in the rejection of, at least, the homogeneity restriction may appear, at first sight, to refute the whole basis of consumer theory. However, it is feasible that non-homogeneity may result from the type of model being used to test for it rather than be a property of the data actually being analysed. If demand systems are to be estimated at all, it is a prerequisite that some quantities be parametrised, i.e. treated as constants which are independent of prices and total expenditure. In log–linear systems all elasticities are parametrised, in the LES subsistence quantities and marginal propensities to spend are treated as constants, while in Rotterdam systems the parameters are the π_{ij} and the μ_i. However, any parametrisation necessarily places restrictions on the functional forms that are used for demand equations, and restrictions on functional form may have unexpected implications. This makes it imperative to distinguish between those findings which are genuinely a reflection of the data under analysis and those which are simply inherent in the model being used. For example, it would be unwise to conclude that no goods are inferior on evidence obtained from the use of a linear expenditure system.

The parametrisation adopted in the Rotterdam model has, similarly, some highly restrictive implications. The model is a differential demand system obtained from equations [2.11A]. However, if the equation system [2.11A] is to be derivable at all from the underlying demand system [2.3A], then a necessary condition is that the partial derivatives $\partial q_i/\partial m$ and $\partial q_i/\partial p_j$ in equation [2.11A] exist and are continuous. However, for this to be so, a well-known result in differential calculus known as *Young's theorem* states that it is necessary that

$$\frac{\partial^2 q_i}{\partial m \, \partial p_j} = \frac{\partial^2 q_i}{\partial p_j \, \partial m} \qquad [2.76]$$

If this so-called 'integrability condition' is not met, it means that equations [2.11A], and hence the Rotterdam system, cannot be derived from equations [2.3A] and therefore can hardly be referred to as a demand system. Unfortunately, if the second-order partial derivatives in equation [2.76] are evaluated *for the Rotterdam case where the μ_i's and the π_{ij}'s in equation [2.32] are assumed to be constant*, then the imposition of the restrictions necessary for equation [2.76] to hold means that the model 'collapses' to a very simple system of demand equations of the form

$$q_i = \mu_i\left(\frac{m}{p_i}\right) \qquad i = 1, 2, 3, \ldots, n \qquad\qquad [2.77]$$

The demand equations [2.77] are known as the *Bergson functions* and were first examined by Bergson (1936). They imply that all total expenditure and own-price elasticities are unity and that all cross-price elasticities are zero. This means that expenditure on any good, $p_i q_i$, is always some constant proportion, μ_i, of total expenditure m regardless of the structure of relative prices. This is clearly an unrealistic description of consumer behaviour. Moreover, the Bergson functions [2.77] are easily shown to arise from the maximisation of the additive utility function $U = \Sigma \beta_i \log q_i$ and hence must *necessarily* satisfy all the restrictions implied by consumer theory. In a moment we shall demonstrate that the Bergson functions imply equations of the Rotterdam form, but first let us consider further the properties of the utility function $U = \Sigma \beta_i \log q_i$.

Homothetic preferences
The utility function $U = \Sigma \beta_i \log q_i$ is an example of what are known as *homothetic utility functions*. The reader will already be familiar with the idea of constant returns to scale in the context of production functions, where equiproportionate changes in all inputs lead to the same equiproportionate change in output. Since utility functions are cardinal, the analogous concept in consumer theory is a little more complex. A utility function is homothetic provided it is a continuous monotonic transformation of a utility function that is homogeneous of degree unity (i.e. that 'produces' utility under conditions of constant returns to scale). Thus, since the utility function $U = \Sigma_i \beta_i \log q_i$ can be written as $U = \alpha \log V$, where $V = \Pi_i q_i^{\beta_i/\alpha}$ and $\alpha = \Sigma \beta_i$, it is homothetic since V is homogeneous of degree unity.

A consumer's preferences are said to be homothetic if one out of the class of utility functions that represent these preferences is homogeneous of degree unity, i.e. produces utility under constant returns to scale. Indifference curves representing homothetic preferences are illustrated in Fig. 2.6 for the two-good case. They are directly analogous to the isoquants of a constant return-to-scale production function except that the labelling of the indifference curves is merely ordinal and not cardinal. Any ray from the origin will cut all indifference curves at points of identical slope.

The shape of the indifference curves in Fig. 2.6 implies that as the consumer's budget line is moved outward in parallel with itself there is no change in the ratio q_1/q_2. Thus the consumer's 'expansion' path if given by $q_1 = kq_2$ where k is a function of the relative price ratio. Substitution in the budget constraint [2.2] then yields the result that, for both goods, the total expenditure elasticity is unity. Thus homothetic preferences imply that at given prices a constant proportion of total expenditure is allocated to each good.[17] The Bergson

2.6 Indifference curves for homothetic preferences

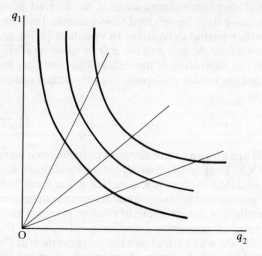

functions [2.77] provide a special case of this. Unfortunately, expenditure proportionality is so much at variance with almost all empirical evidence that the concept of homothetic preferences is of little practical use.

It is not difficult to show that the Bergson functions [2.77] imply differential demand equations of the Rotterdam form which have constant μ_i's and π_{ij}'s. For example, consider the first demand equation in the simple two-good case. The Bergson function is $q_1 = \mu_1(m/p_1)$ and since μ_1 is a constant we have that $w_1 = \mu_1$, i.e. the average and marginal propensities to spend are the same and constant. Using the first equation in [2.11] and multiplying throughout by p_1/m yields

$$w_1 \, d \log q_1 = \mu_1 \, d \log m - \mu_1 \, d \log p_1 \qquad [2.78]$$

where we have also used the first equation in [2.14] which in this case reduces to $p_1(\partial q_1/\partial p_1) = -q_1$. Since the utility function

From the definition of the π_{ij} (given below equation [2.32]) we have that

$$\pi_{11} = \frac{p_1^2}{m}\left[\frac{\partial q_1}{\partial p_1} + q_1 \frac{\partial q_1}{\partial m}\right] = -\mu_1 + \mu_1^2$$

and

$$\pi_{12} = \frac{p_1 p_2}{m}\left[\frac{\partial q_1}{\partial p_2} + q_2 \frac{\partial q_1}{\partial m}\right] = \mu_1 \mu_2$$

Hence we can write [2.78] as

$$
\begin{aligned}
w_1 \, d \log q_1 &= \mu_1 \, d \log m - (\mu_1^2 - \pi_{11}) \, d \log p_1 - (\mu_1 \mu_2 - \pi_{12}) \, d \log p_2 \\
&= \mu_1 \, d \log m - (\mu_1 w_1 - \pi_{11}) \, d \log p_1 \\
&\quad - (\mu_1 w_2 - \pi_{12}) \, d \log p_2 \\
&= \mu_1[d \log m - \sum w_j \, d \log p_j] + \sum \pi_{1j} \, d \log p_j \\
&= \mu_1 \sum w_j \, d \log q_j + \sum \pi_{1j} \, d \log p_j
\end{aligned}
$$

which is the first equation in a two-equation Rotterdam model. Similarly, the Bergson function $q_2 = \mu_2(m/p_2)$ reduces to the second equation in such a model. The important point is that the converse result is also true. If the integrability condition [2.76] is imposed, then if we start with the 'constant coefficients' version of the Rotterdam model we are led inexorably back to demand equations in the levels which are of the same implausible Bergson form. This converse result was originally derived by D. McFadden in an unpublished paper but a proof is provided in, for example, Theil (1975).

The 'expenditure proportionality' implications of the Rotterdam model seem to seriously restrict its usefulness as a completely general system of demand equations. If the model implies a demand system which automatically satisfies all the theoretical restrictions, it can hardly be used to test these restrictions. However, empirical versions of the Rotterdam model necessarily use finite log differences such as $\log q_{it} - \log q_{it-1}$, as approximations to the log differentials of equation [2.32]. It is certainly not true that the estimates of total expenditure and own-price elasticities obtained in this manner are invariably unity, as implied by the Bergson functions. The Rotterdam school in fact reply to the above criticism by pointing out that their system can be derived as the first terms of a Taylor approximation to *any* arbitrary demand system (see, for example, Theil 1975). Since the system is designed to approximate first-order changes only, second-order derivatives such as those involved in equation [2.76] are not relevant. However, the first terms of such a Taylor expansion can only provide close approximations when changes in the variables involved are relatively small. This is unfortunate because if precise estimates of the parameters of any model are to be obtained we require large variations in its variables.

The upshot of the above is that the Rotterdam model is, at best, an approximation (although maybe a good one) to the true demand system, whatever that may be. Since it is merely an approximation, this is one possible reason why its use tends to lead to the rejection of the homogeneity restriction. Although the true demand system is homogeneous, the best Rotterdam approximation over most sample periods *could just be* non-homogeneous. As we shall see, however, there are more compelling explanations than this for the apparent failure of data to comply with homogeneity.

Other early models of demand

We begin by considering a model which bears comparison with the LES in that it makes specific assumptions about the consumer's preference ordering and leads to demand equations which automatically satisfy all the general restrictions of consumer theory. This is the *indirect addilog model* of Houthakker (1960).

Houthakker begins with the indirect utility function. We have seen that, given a specific functional form for the cost function, it is possible to generate Hicksian and Marshallian demand functions. Similarly, given a specific indirect utility function we can generate Marshallian demands. This is done by using 'Roy's identity' which states that[18]

$$q_i = \frac{\partial U^*/\partial p_i}{\partial U^*/\partial m} \qquad [2.79]$$

Thus, by the use of equation [2.79], *any* function which is homogeneous of degree zero in prices and total expenditure (and hence can be regarded as an indirect utility function) may be utilised to generate demand equations consistent with all the restrictions of consumer theory. Houthakker considers the case where the indirect utility function is written as an additive function of the ratios of prices to total expenditure and takes the specific form

$$U^* = \frac{\alpha_1}{\beta_1}\left(\frac{p_1}{m}\right)^{\beta_1} + \frac{\alpha_2}{\beta_2}\left(\frac{p_2}{m}\right)^{\beta_2} + \cdots + \frac{\alpha_n}{\beta_n}\left(\frac{p_n}{m}\right)^{\beta_n} \qquad [2.80]$$

Applying Roy's identity to equation [2.80] and taking logarithms yields the demand equations

$$\log q_i = \log \alpha_i + (\beta_i + 1) \log \left(\frac{m}{p_i}\right) + \log \left[\sum_k \alpha_k \left(\frac{m}{p_k}\right)^{\beta_k}\right] \qquad [2.81]$$

One interesting point about the demand system [2.81] is that Houthakker originally obtained this specification by beginning with the double logarithmic demand system [2.30] and then transforming it in such a way that the aggregation and other general restrictions were satisfied. Thus, just as imposing the general restrictions on a linear demand system leads to the LES, the imposition of these restrictions on the double-log model leads to the indirect addilog system [2.81].

The indirect addilog model is slightly more flexible than the LES in that, depending on the size of the β_i parameters, inferior goods are possible as is Hicksian complementarity. However, when direct comparisons between the models were made the indirect addilog model appeared to fit the data worse than the LES. Moreover, the computational problems of estimation are greater than for the LES, although the non-linearity of equation [2.81] may be circumvented by considering the ratios of demands for pairs of goods:

$$\log q_i - \log q_j = \log \alpha_i - \log \alpha_j + (\beta_i + 1) \log \left(\frac{m}{p_i}\right)$$
$$- (\beta_j + 1) \log \left(\frac{m}{p_j}\right) \qquad [2.82]$$

Houthakker also suggested a model where the *direct* utility function takes the additive form

$$U = \left(\frac{\alpha_1}{\beta_1}\right) q_1^{\beta_1} + \left(\frac{\alpha_2}{\beta_2}\right) q_2^{\beta_2} + \cdots + \left(\frac{\alpha_n}{\beta_n}\right) q_n^{\beta_n} \qquad [2.83]$$

Maximisation of such a utility function leads to demand equations bearing an obvious resemblance to those of [2.82].

$$(\beta_i - 1) \log q_i - (\beta_j - 1) \log q_j = \log p_i - \log p_j - \log \left(\frac{\alpha_i}{\alpha_j}\right) \qquad [2.84]$$

However, apart from its original use by Houthakker this *direct addilog* model has been little used in applied work.

Of demand systems which do not necessarily satisfy the theoretical restrictions and hence may be used for testing them, the simplest used in applied work has been the double logarithmic system [2.30] which treats the elasticities as parameters. We have already noted that, when expressed in terms of elasticities, the general theoretical restrictions vary with levels of prices and total expenditure and hence will not be constant over time. The model is therefore unable to fully satisfy the restrictions of theory. Investigators, however, generally tested or imposed the theoretical restrictions at one particular point, normally the point of mean budget shares, since the budget shares, w_i, are the items which appear in the restrictions when they are expressed in terms of elasticities. It was assumed that the restrictions will be approximately satisfied at other points.

Results with this model tended to duplicate those obtained with the Rotterdam model. For example, studies by Byron (1970a) and (1970b) both led to the rejection of the homogeneity and symmetry restrictions. However, the fact that the theoretical restrictions cannot be fully satisfied by this model means that, like the Rotterdam model, it is at best an approximation and in this case the approximation leads to some strange results. Byron used Barten's Dutch data for sixteen commodity groupings. Since the data 'add up' in the sense that they satisfy the budget constraint for all observations, the aggregation restrictions should necessarily be satisfied. Yet Byron's tests led to the rejection of the Engel aggregation restriction [2.13B]! As Byron pointed out, this rejection had to be the result of the model used rather than any defect in consumer theory. This result highlights the necessity, noted during our discussion of the Rotterdam model, of where possible making a clear distinction between findings which genuinely represent properties of the data under analysis and those which are simply a reflection of the model in use.

2.7   Flexible functional forms

The disadvantages of adopting one or other of the approaches outlined at the beginning of the previous section naturally suggests an attempt to combine the two. This has led more recently to attempts to approximate utility functions (direct or indirect) and cost functions by so-called *flexible functional forms*. These flexible forms must, firstly, contain sufficient parameters to be regarded as an adequate approximation to whatever the 'true' underlying utility or cost function happens to be. Secondly, they must generate demand equations which are capable of satisfying, but do not necessarily satisfy, the general restrictions of theory. Thus they can be used for the testing of theory, but the demand equations obtained do not have any unforeseen implications for the underlying preference ordering. The first major attempt along these lines was that of Christensen *et al.* (1975). In one of their two specifications – the direct translog model – they approximate the negative of the logarithm of the direct utility function by a function which is quadratic in the logarithms of the quantities consumed:

$$-\log U = \alpha_0 + \sum_i \alpha_i \log q_i + \tfrac{1}{2} \sum_i \sum_j \beta_{ij} \log q_i \log q_j \qquad [2.85]$$

Equation [2.85] contains enough parameters to be regarded as a 'local second-order approximation' to any arbitrary direct utility function. To see what is meant by this consider the two-good case where [2.85] becomes

$$-\log U = \alpha_0 + \alpha_1 \log q_1 + \alpha_2 \log q_2 + \tfrac{1}{2}\beta_{11}(\log q_1)^2 + \tfrac{1}{2}\beta_{22}(\log q_2)^2$$
$$+ \tfrac{1}{2}(\beta_{12} + \beta_{21}) \log q_1 \log q_2$$

The first- and second-order derivatives of the utility function are in this case

$$\frac{\partial \log U}{\partial \log q_1} = -\alpha_1 - \beta_{11} \log q_1 - \beta_{12} \log q_2$$

$$\frac{\partial \log U}{\partial \log q_2} = -\alpha_2 - \beta_{22} \log q_2 - \beta_{21} \log q_1$$

$$\frac{\partial^2 \log U}{\partial(\log q_1)^2} = -\beta_{11} \qquad \frac{\partial^2 \log U}{\partial(\log q_2)^2} = -\beta_{22}$$

$$\frac{\partial^2 \log U}{\partial(\log q_1)\,\partial(\log q_2)} = \frac{\partial^2 \log U}{\partial(\log q_2)\,\partial(\log q_1)} = -\beta_{12}$$

where we have set $\beta_{12} = \beta_{21}$ without any loss of generality. The above represent five equations in the five parameters α_1, α_2, β_{11}, β_{22} and $\beta_{12} = \beta_{21}$. Hence, for any selected values of q_1 and q_2 we can choose these parameters so as to make the above first and second derivatives equal to those of any arbitrary utility function. Also, for any values of q_1 and q_2 in the neighbourhood of their selected values we will still have a good 'second-order approximation' of the arbitrary utility function. Since this is the case for any arbitrary utility function, it must be so for the true, underlying utility function, whatever that may be

Maximisation of the utility function [2.85] subject to the usual budget constraint leads to equations for the budget shares of each good of the form

$$w_i = \frac{\alpha_i + \Sigma_j \, \beta_{ij} \log q_j}{\alpha_m + \Sigma_j \, \beta_{mj} \log q_j} \qquad i = 1, 2, 3, \ldots, n \qquad [2.86]$$

where $\alpha_m = \Sigma_i \alpha_i$ and $\beta_{mj} = \Sigma_i \beta_{ij}$.

In their other specification, the *indirect translog model*, Christiansen, Jorgenson and Lau approximate the logarithm of the indirect utility function by a function which is quadratic in the logarithms of the ratios of prices to total expenditure:

$$\log U^* = \alpha_0' + \sum_i \alpha_i' \log\left(\frac{p_i}{m}\right) + \tfrac{1}{2} \sum_i \sum_j \beta_{ij} \log\left(\frac{p_i}{m}\right) \log\left(\frac{p_j}{m}\right)$$

$$[2.87]$$

Just as [2.85] provides a local second-order approximation to any direct utility function, [2.87] contains enough parameters to provide such an approximation to any indirect utility function in the neighbourhood of any given set of p_i/m ratios.

Via Roy's identity (see equation [2.79]) the following equations for the budget shares can be obtained from [2.87]:

$$w_i = \frac{\alpha_i' + \Sigma_j \, \beta_{ij}' \log (p_j/m)}{\alpha_m' + \Sigma_j \, \beta_{mj}' \log (p_j/m)} \qquad i = 1, 2, 3, \ldots, n \qquad [2.88]$$

where $\alpha_m' = \Sigma_i \alpha_i'$ and $\beta_{mj}' = \Sigma_i \beta_{ij}'$.

Notice that the systems of equations [2.86] and [2.88], if estimated without any restrictions imposed, are capable of satisfying restrictions consistent with utility maximisation but will not necessarily do so. For example, if equations

[2.86] are generated by utility maximisation then the β_{mj} parameters that appear in each equation must be the same. However, if equations [2.86] are freely estimated there is no reason why all the β_{mj} should be the same, unless of course the equations are the result of utility maximisation.

The authors argue that since [2.85] and [2.87] can be regarded as second-order approximations to *any* direct or indirect utility function, data *must* conform to the demand systems [2.86] and [2.88] (together with the restrictions they imply) if consumer theory is to be regarded as valid. They use maximum likelihood methods to estimate their system for US annual data for 1929–72 using three commodity groupings – non-durable consumption goods, services from durable consumption goods and other services. They conclude that their results 'make possible an unambiguous rejection of the theory of demand'. Such a conclusion, however, is rather premature and could only be acceptable if the direct utility function were exactly of the form [2.85] or if the indirect utility function were exactly of the form [2.87]. However, [2.85] and [2.87] are merely approximations (whether good or bad) to the true utility functions so that a rejection of consumer theory on the basis of the translog models is no more final than a rejection on the basis of the Rotterdam or double-log models. What is more convincing, of course, is that *all* three models, each using different approximations, come up with exactly the same result – that the restrictions implied by consumer theory do not hold.

The almost ideal demand system

An alternative to using a flexible functional form to approximate the direct or indirect utility function is, of course, to use such a form to approximate the cost function. One good reason for attempting to approximate the cost function is that, as we have seen, by adopting this approach we are not restricted to considering only convex consumer preference orderings. Deaton and Muellbauer (1980b) in their *Almost Ideal Demand System* (AIDS) adopt the following flexible functional form for the cost-function of an individual house-hold h.

$$\log m^h = \alpha_0 + \log k^h + \sum_i \alpha_i \log p_i + \tfrac{1}{2} \sum_i \sum_j \gamma_{ij}^* \log p_i \log p_j$$
$$+ U^h \beta_0 \prod_j p_j^{\beta_j} \qquad [2.89]$$

Equation [2.89] will be homogeneous of degree unity in prices (as it must be if it is to be regarded as a cost function) provided $\Sigma_i \alpha_i = 1$ and $\Sigma_i \gamma_{ij}^* = \Sigma_j \gamma_{ij}^* = \Sigma_j \beta_j = 0$. Two points are to be noted concerning the cost function [2.89]. Firstly, it contains sufficient parameters for its first- and second-order derivatives to be set equal to those of any arbitrary cost function. Secondly, it belongs to the PIGLOG family of cost functions described at the end of Section 2.5, the general form of which was given by equation [2.63A]. The b_1 and b_2 functions of [2.63A] are in the AIDS case given by

$$\log b_1(p) = \alpha_0 + \sum_i \alpha_i \log p_i + \tfrac{1}{2} \sum_i \sum_j \gamma_{ij}^* \log p_i \log p_j \qquad [2.90]$$

$$\log b_2(p) = \log b_1(p) + \beta_0 \prod_j p_j^{\beta_j} \qquad [2.91]$$

Equations for the budget shares of each good can be obtained from [2.89] by firstly using the logarithmic version of Shephard's lemma,

$$w_i = \frac{\partial \log m}{\partial \log p_i}$$

and then substituting for U^h using the indirect utility function. Remember that the indirect utility function can be obtained, simply by rearranging the cost function [2.89] to express U^h in terms of m and the p_i. The budget share equations for household h are

$$w_i^h = \alpha_i + \sum_j \gamma_{ij} \log p_j + \beta_i \log \left(\frac{m^h}{k^h P} \right) \qquad i = 1, 2, 3, \ldots, n \qquad [2.92]$$

where P is an index of prices defined by

$$\log P = \alpha_0 + \sum_i \alpha_i \log p_i + \tfrac{1}{2} \sum_i \sum_j \gamma_{ij} \log p_i \log p_j \qquad [2.93]$$

and the γ_{ij} are defined as

$$\gamma_{ij} = \tfrac{1}{2}(\gamma_{ij}^* + \gamma_{ji}^*) = \gamma_{ji} \qquad [2.94]$$

Equations [2.92] represent the AIDS and Deaton and Muellbauer are able to claim a number of advantages for it. Firstly, not only can the cost function [2.89] be regarded as a local second-order approximation to the underlying cost function, whatever that should be, but the budget share equations [2.92] contain sufficient parameters to be regarded as a local first-order approximation to any demand system. From [2.92]

$$\frac{\partial w_i^h}{\partial \log m^h} = \beta_i \quad \text{and} \quad \frac{\partial w_i^h}{\partial \log p_j} = \gamma_{ij} - \beta_i \alpha_j - \beta_i \sum_k \gamma_{jk} \log p_k$$

so that if the α's are treated simply as intercepts, then at any point the β's and γ's can be chosen so as to make the first-order derivatives of the AIDS identical to those of the true model whether that model is consistent with consumer theory or not. The cost function approximation therefore makes the AIDS as general as the translog model, while the demand system approximation makes it also as general as the Rotterdam model.

As with the Rotterdam model, the general restrictions of consumer theory are unchanged for all values of total expenditure and prices and can be expressed entirely in terms of the parameters of the budget share equations [2.92]. This makes the AIDS a suitable vehicle for the testing of these restrictions. The aggregation restrictions require that for all j,

$$\sum_i \alpha_i = 1, \quad \sum_i \beta_i = 0, \quad \sum_i \gamma_{ij} = 0$$

while homogeneity requires that $\Sigma_j \gamma_{ij} = 0$ for all i. These restrictions follow from the requirement that the cost function [2.89] be homogeneous of degree unity in prices. The symmetry restriction is satisfied provided that $\gamma_{ij} = \gamma_{ji}$. This follows from equation [2.94]. As with the Rotterdam model, there is no guarantee that these restrictions will be satisfied if equations [2.92] are freely estimated. Hence if the restrictions are not rejected by available data, this can be taken as evidence in favour of the theory of consumer behaviour.

A further major advantage of AIDS is that, since the cost function [2.89] belongs to the PIGLOG class, the budget share equations [2.92] can be perfectly aggregated and the aggregate equations obtained can also be expected to obey the above restrictions. The aggregate equations should, strictly speaking, involve representative expenditure rather than mean expenditure, where representative expenditure, m_0, is given by equation [2.67]. However, using the arguments below [2.67] we can relate representative expenditure to mean expenditure, $\bar{m}$ by introducing the aggregate index k. This index will remain constant over time provided the distributions of household tastes and household total expenditures remain unchanged. We can therefore write aggregate budget share equations in the form [2.68], or, for the AIDS case,

$$\bar{w}_i = \alpha_i + \sum_j \gamma_{ij} \log p_j + \beta_i \log \left(\frac{\bar{m}}{kP} \right) \qquad [2.95]$$

where P is the general price index defined previously.

Deaton and Muellbauer also point out that for cross-sectional data, where prices can be regarded as constant, the equations [2.92] reduce to

$$w_i^h = a_{0i} + a_{1i} \log \left(\frac{m^h}{k^h} \right)$$

where a_{0i} and a_{1i} are functions of the constant prices. Thus like all PIGLOG models, but unlike many previous time series models, the AIDS implies non-linear Engel curves. We have seen in Section 1.5 that most cross-sectional studies have supported the idea of non-linear Engel curves, while at the end of Section 2.5 we noted that the above functional form, implied by the AIDS, is well known for its ability to provide close fits to most cross-sectional data.

The final important advantage that can be claimed for the AIDS is that of ease of estimation. Given P, equation [2.95] is linear in the parameters. Since prices tend to move collinearly over time, a good approximation to P is given by a price index such as $\Sigma_i \, w_i \log p_i$, which may be calculated prior to the estimation process. Thus, provided it is not required to enforce the cross-equation symmetry restriction, the AIDS may be estimated equation by equation using, for example, ordinary least squares. The simplicity of equations [2.95] is in sharp contrast to the translog equations for budget shares [2.86] and [2.88]. If an adequate approximation for P is not possible, or it is wished to impose symmetry, then estimation is less easy and maximum likelihood methods involving non-linear estimation are necessary.

Deaton and Muellbauer estimate their model using annual British data for 1954–74 on eight non-durable commodity groups – food, clothing, housing services, fuel, drink and tobacco, transport and communication services, other goods and other services. If the index k in equation [2.95] is treated as a constant, this equation can be written as[19]

$$\bar{w}_i = (\alpha_i - \beta_i \log k) + \sum_j \gamma_{ij} \log p_j + \beta_i \log \left(\frac{\bar{m}}{P} \right) \qquad [2.96]$$

and this is the form estimated, the $\beta_i \log k$ term being incorporated into the intercept. Notice that it is not possible to include representative expenditure, m_0, in the estimating equation as the aggregate theory suggests because the individual household m^h's required if equation [2.67] is to be evaluated are, of course, unknown. Hence the need to make use of the relationship $\bar{m} = km_0$.

Deaton and Muellbauer find that for four of their commodity groups – food, clothing, housing services and transport – the homogeneity restriction is rejected. The cross-equation symmetry restrictions are also rejected and, moreover, in contrast to some previous studies (e.g. Deaton 1974a), symmetry is rejected whether or not the maintained hypothesis includes homogeneity. Thus yet again we appear to arrive at the conclusion that available data are inconsistent with consumer theory. Of course, the AIDS involves approximations, but we can now list four models – Rotterdam, log–linear, translog and AIDS – all making use of different approximations but all producing the same result: an apparent rejection of consumer theory.

2.8   Outstanding problems

The apparent consistency with which empirical studies arrive at a rejection of the homogeneity and symmetry restrictions may, at first glance, appear to be impressive. However, it would be most rash at this stage to reject, out of hand, the whole basis of consumer theory. Applied demand studies in general have paid little or no attention to a whole range of problems which, potentially, may invalidate many of the results obtained.

Firstly, in our discussion of the single-equation approach to demand analysis we paid particular attention in Section 1.3 to the problems of identification and simultaneity. In the complete system approach these problems tend to be almost totally ignored. This is presumably because estimation is sufficiently complex (especially when cross-equation restrictions are to be imposed) even without allowing for joint endogeneity in the determination of prices and quantities. Even if identification poses no problem, the likelihood of simultaneous equation bias can only be safely ignored if it can be assumed that prices are set exogenously and that quantities are in infinitely elastic supply. While this may not be an unreasonable assumption for many 'manufactured' goods in an industrial society, it is by no means clear that it will hold for many foodstuffs. Recently Bronsard and Salvas-Bronsard (1984) have attempted to test the assumption of price exogeneity. A comparison of models with endogenous and models with exogenous prices suggests that the assumption of price exogeneity is 'not a dramatic one'. Results for both types of models turn out to be very similar. However, this problem is nowhere near resolved.

Secondly, total expenditure may not be the appropriate choice of exogenous variable, even for the individual household. Obviously not all income is spent on current expenditure – many households have high propensities to save. We have seen that it may well be possible to adopt a multi-stage budgeting approach to a household's problem of intertemporal choice. It is then justifiable to express demand as a function of total *current* expenditure. However, total income itself may not be exogenous. To the extent that a household is able to vary the number of hours it works, it gains control over its own income.

The neo-classical theory of labour supply handles this situation by including leisure, L, in the household's utility function in addition to all the goods it consumes:

$$U = U(q_1, q_2, q_3, \ldots, q_n, L) \tag{2.97}$$

If the household faces a constant wage rate, w, and the total 'time available' for work is T then the household's total income becomes $m + w(T - L)$ where m is its non-wage income. The budget constraint facing the household is therefore

$$\sum_i p_i q_i = m + w(T - L) \qquad [2.98]$$

which we may write as

$$\sum_i p_i q_i + wL = m + wT \qquad [2.99]$$

We have reformulated the problem so that it is now similar to the usual type of consumer choice problem with w playing the role of the 'price' of the 'good' leisure. Maximisation of the utility function [2.97] subject to [2.99] leads to demand equations for all goods including leisure. Since the hours a household chooses to work are given by $T - L$, the demand for leisure equation is, of course, an implicit supply of labour equation. Notice, however, that in this problem it is the wage rate rather than household income or total expenditure which is the exogenous variable. Also the wage rate appears in the budget constraint [2.99] not only as the price of leisure but also as a determinant of household income. This has implications for, and in fact complicates, the analysis of income and substitution effects.

An important aspect of the neo-classical labour supply model concerns the 'participation decision' – that is, the decision of a household whether actually to supply a positive number of hours of work or not to work at all. Suppose the household purchases just one good, so that its budget constraint becomes $pq + wL = m + wT$ where p and q are the price and quantity purchased of the good. This budget constraint is given by ABC in Fig. 2.7. The distance OC equals T, the total time available for work, so that if $L = OC$ then no hours are supplied and the household's total real income is only CB which equals m/p. However, if L equals zero then all of T is devoted to work and real income is OA which equals $(m/p) + (w/p)T$.

Two types of equilibrium are now possible. Firstly, equilibrium could occur at a point such as E where the budget line is tangential to one of the indifference

2.7 The participation decision

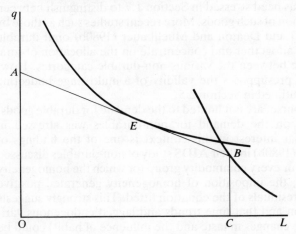

curves representing the household's preferences between consumption and leisure. Secondly, if the indifference curves were more steeply sloped, we could get a 'corner solution' at B where the household supplies no hours of labour at all. Clearly the latter type of equilibrium could not be found using normal differential calculus methods.

Once it is accepted that the demand for goods and the supply of labour are inextricably entangled, additional problems arise. For example, most workers do not have complete control over the number of hours they work – for many the choice may be between working a fixed number of hours per week or not working at all. In addition, the shape of a household's budget constraint may be further complicated by the precise form of the tax and social security system under which it operates. For example, since marginal tax rates tend to rise with income, this introduces quite complex non-linearities into budget constraints. Any such non-linearities, of course, severely complicate the estimation process.

If the demand for goods and the supply of labour are regarded as part of the same overall maximisation problem then this has interesting consequences for the estimation of Engel curves from cross-sectional data. It is usually assumed that prices can be regarded as constant over a single cross-section. However, it is clear that no such assumption can be made regarding the wage rate. Blundell (1980) uses this fact to overcome the problem (mentioned in Section 1.5) that, when estimating consumer expenditure scales, the parameters of household composition functions are generally unidentified. The problem arose partly because of the lack of variation in prices over the cross-section. Blundell treats a household's demand for goods and supply of labour as jointly determined and this leads to the introduction of a non-constant price (the wage rate) into an otherwise conventional demand system. This helps to identify the underlying household composition parameters.

Dynamic factors

Finally, perhaps the most serious deficiency of applied work has been the general failure in the past to treat expenditure on durable goods as any different from that on non-durables. Many studies such as Barten (1969) and Deaton (1974a) treated durable goods as a commodity grouping no different from any other, despite the obvious need stressed in Section 1.7 to distinguish between purchases and consumption of such goods. More recent studies such as those by Christensen *et al.* (1975) and Deaton and Muellbauer (1980b) omit durable goods from the analysis altogether and concentrate on the allocation of total non-durable expenditure between the various non-durable categories. However, such an approach presupposes the validity of a multi-stage budgeting procedure such as that outlined in Section 2.5.

Dynamic factors, of course, are not limited to the demand for durable goods. The influence of habit on the demand for non-durables was stressed in Section 1.7. Of particular interest in this context is one of the findings of Deaton and Muellbauer (1980b) in their AIDS study of non-durables discussed above. They found that for every commodity group for which the homogeneity restriction was rejected, the imposition of homogeneity generated positive serial correlation in the residuals of the equation fitted. This strongly suggests dynamic mis-specification and that time trends and lagged endogenous variables (reflecting, maybe, changes in taste and the influence of habit) could be omitted variables in the model. In addition, when Deaton and Muellbauer estimated their equations in 'first difference' form, the inclusion of a constant term (the equivalent of including a time trend in a 'levels' equation) led to improved results with less frequent rejections of homogeneity. Dynamic mis-specification, leading to biased estimates of price and total expenditure coefficients, is therefore another plausible explanation for the rejection of the homogeneity and symmetry restrictions.

Attempts to introduce dynamic factors into empirical studies date back to the earliest attempts to estimate complete systems of demand equations. However, as with the single-equation studies discussed in Section 1.7, many of these attempts have been largely of an *an hoc* nature, often involving no more than the addition of time trends to already specified demand equations. A more promising approach is to attempt to dynamise the utility function rather than the demand equations themselves. There are two possible advantages in such an approach. Firstly, the resultant demand equations will necessarily be capable of satisfying the general theoretical restrictions. Secondly, as we observed in the single-equation context, it would be more satisfactory if the state adjustment processes outlined there could be seen to arise from some maximisation process carried out by the consumer. The possibility arises of specifying the dynamic utility function such that the resultant demand system does incorporate such processes.

One method of dynamising the utility function is to make its parameters functions of time. Such an approach was adopted as early as 1966 by Stone who, in a dynamic version of the LES made the β and γ parameters linear or quadratic functions of a time trend. Alternatively, the β and γ parameters could be made functions of past purchases. Such a system was in fact estimated by Pollak and Wales (1969). A further possibility is to introduce stock variables into the utility function by making its parameters dependent on stocks – stocks of durable goods or stocks of 'habits'. Examples of this type of model are Phlips' (1972) dynamic linear expenditure system in which the γ parameters are made functions of stocks held, and the dynamic model of Houthakker and Taylor (1970) where the utility function is assumed to be quadratic in purchases and stocks held. An interesting feature of these models is that the resultant demand equations do incorporate the state adjustment processes mentioned earlier. In fact, it can be shown that Phlips' utility function is the only such dynamic utility function that leads to a system of linear demand equations in which state variables are included.

More recent attempts to introduce dynamic elements into demand models include those of Blanciforti and Green (1983), who introduce habit effects into the Deaton–Muellbauer AIDS model, and Anderson and Blundell (1983) and (1984). The latter use the AIDS model to describe long-run behaviour but non-symmetric and non-homogeneous short-run behaviour is permitted. The symmetry and homogeneity restrictions are only expected to hold in steady state. Dynamic AIDS equations of the following type are estimated:

$$\Delta w_{it} = \sum_j c_{ij} \, \mathrm{d} \log p_{jt} + b_i \, \mathrm{d} \log \left(\frac{m}{p} \right)_t -$$

$$- \lambda \left[w_{it-1} - \sum_j \gamma_{ij} \log p_{jt-1} - \beta_i \log \left(\frac{m}{p} \right)_{t-1} \right] \qquad [2.100]$$

Thus, current changes in budget shares depend not only on current changes in the normal AIDS explanatory variables but also on the extent of consumer disequilibrium in the previous period. In steady state, however, equation [2.100] reduces to a normal AIDS equation. The methodology is similar to that of, for example, Davidson *et al.* (1978) and is now regularly used in the study of the determinants of aggregate consumer expenditure.

In their 1983 study, Anderson and Blundell apply their model to annual Canadian data on five categories of non-durable goods for 1947–79. The 1984 study deals with quarterly UK data on four categories of non-durables for 1955–81. Results are substantially the same in both cases. The static AIDS model is rejected in favour of the above dynamic version. Moreover, the dynamic model proves superior both to the static model with autocorrelated error term and to a simple habit persistence–partial adjustment type of dynamic model.

The results also indicate that the restrictions of symmetry and homogeneity are not rejected *when imposed on the long-run or steady-state structure of the model*. This suggests that previous rejections of symmetry and homogeneity are indeed the result of mis-specifications that are inherent in purely static models.

As with single-equation models, little attention has been paid so far to consumer expectations. As we saw in Section 1.7, the neo-classical approach to the demand for durables highlights the importance of expected future prices on the timing of purchases. Such factors have yet to be allowed for in the full system approach to empirical demand analysis. Furthermore, in a truly dynamic model account must be taken of a consumer's ability to finance current purchases. This is another important influence on the timing of purchases. Restrictions on borrowing, government imposed or otherwise, then become relevant.

Finally, it has to be remembered that systems such as the Rotterdam model, the translog systems and the AIDS are all approximations to the true demand system, whatever that happens to be. This raises the interesting question of which system provides the best approximation under any given set of conditions. Byron (1984) has made a start to answering such questions. He considers how well the Rotterdam model is able to reproduce the characteristics of four integratable demand systems. In a simulation study he found that bias in the parameters was minimal for three of the systems but that the Rotterdam approximation was (not surprisingly) suspect for a model which implied that the quantities parametrised in the Rotterdam system were non-constant.

The next decade will almost certainly see much further work on the estimation of complete systems of demand equations. All the questions raised in this section require further examination. In particular, attention is likely to be concentrated on dynamic models in general and on the integration of such models with labour supply theory.

Notes

1. We adopt the notation $U_i = \partial U / \partial q_i$ for the first-order derivatives of the utility function and $U_{ij} = \partial^2 U / (\partial q_i \, \partial q_j)$ for the second-order derivatives.

2. We in fact assume a twice differentiable strictly quasi-concave utility function with positive first derivatives. This also implies that the Hessian matrix of second-order partial derivatives of the utility function, i.e. the matrix $\begin{pmatrix} U_{11} & U_{12} \\ U_{21} & U_{22} \end{pmatrix}$ is negative semi-definite. This ensures that the 'second-order conditions' are met and that we obtain a point of maximum rather than minimum utility.

3. It is implicitly assumed that preferences obey the axioms of 'comparability', 'transitivity', 'continuity' and 'dominance' or 'non-satiation'. See, for example, Phlips (1974, Ch. 1).

4. Indifference curves without linear segments can also have kinks of course.

5. The obvious analogy is that of a firm which can be considered as either choosing its inputs so as to maximise output subject to a cost constraint or as choosing its inputs so as to minimise costs subject to a constraint on output.

6. It is directly analogous to a firm's cost function which expresses the minimum cost of producing a given output at given factor prices.

7. [2.13] is sometimes referred to as the condition for Engel aggregation and [2.14] as the condition for Cournot aggregation.

8. That is, the matrix $\begin{pmatrix} U_{11} & U_{12} \\ U_{21} & U_{22} \end{pmatrix}$.

9. For a proof of 'negativity' in the general n good case see, for example, Phlips (1974, p. 52).

10. If $U_{ij} \neq 0$ this implies that U_i is dependent on q_j, i.e. that the marginal utility of the ith good is dependent on the quantity consumed of the jth good.

11. It should perhaps be stressed that we are not necessarily assuming that the consumer actually behaves in this manner, even though he or she well might do. Multi-stage budgeting merely implies that the consumer's problem can be represented in this manner.

12. Similarly, the quantity $\phi = \dfrac{\mu}{m} = \dfrac{-\lambda/m}{\partial\lambda/\partial m}$ which is sometimes used as a welfare measure cannot be unambiguously interpreted as the reciprocal of the elasticity of the marginal utility of expenditure with respect to expenditure.

13. The preferences referred to should not be regarded as the outcome of 'social choice' in any sense.

14. In the more general PIGL case, the degree of non-linearity in the Engel curves is determined by the parameter α. The budget share equation arising out of [2.63] is $w_i^h = a_{0i} + a_{1i}(m^h/k^h)^{-\alpha}$. Thus for the case $k^h = 1$ for all households, the implied Engel curve is $p_i q_i^h = a_{0i} m^h + a_{1i}(m^h)^{1-\alpha}$ which for $\alpha = 1$ is linear, for $\alpha = -1$ is quadratic, etc.

15. See, for example, Phlips (1974), pp. 122–5.

16. The most extensive use of the Rotterdam model was that by Theil in his two-volume work (1975 and 1976).

17. Homothetic preferences therefore imply linear Engel curves passing through the origin. The cost function associated with the 'constant returns to scale' representation of homothetic preferences must take the form $m =$

$Ub_2(p)$ since if a doubling of utility requires a doubling of all purchases it must also lead to a doubling of costs. Such a cost function may be generalised by adding a fixed cost element to the cost function which then becomes $m = b_1(p) + Ub_2(p)$. The preferences underlying such a cost function are referred to as *quasi-homothetic*. From our discussion of aggregation over consumers, we know that such a cost function also implies linear Engel curves but not this time passing through the origin.

18. See Appendix B.
19. Even if k is not constant over time, provided k is uncorrelated with $\bar{m}$ and P, no bias arises in the estimation of the parameters in equation [2.96].

Appendix A

Concave functions and convex preferences

Concave functions

Suppose, firstly, that z is a function of just one variable, i.e. $z = f[x]$. Such a function is concave if 'looking upwards' from the x-axis it appears concave. This is illustrated in Fig. A.1. Formally $f[x]$ is *concave* if

$$f[\lambda x_1 + (1 - \lambda)x_2] \geqslant \lambda f[x_1] + (1 - \lambda)f[x_2] \qquad \text{[A.1]}$$

where x_1 and x_2 are any given values of x and λ is any constant between 0 and 1. The function is said to be *strictly concave* if a strict inequality sign ($>$) holds in equation [A.1].

The definition can be best understood if we consider the line segment AB in Fig. A.1. Point A has coordinates $(x_1, f[x_1])$ and point B has coordinates $(x_2, f[x_2])$. A point C on the line segment AB will have x-coordinate, $\lambda x_1 + (1 - \lambda)x_2$, and z-coordinate $\lambda f[x_1] + (1 - \lambda)f[x_2]$ where λ is some constant between 0 and 1. That is, C's coordinates are a weighted average of those of A and B. Equation [A.1] with the strict inequality holding, therefore implies that any point such as C must lie below the corresponding point on the function, D, that has the same x-coordinate as C – that is, the function is concave when 'looking upwards' from the x-axis.

The definition can be extended to the case where z is a function of n variables. In this general case concavity has implications for the shape of the function in

A.1 A concave function of one variable

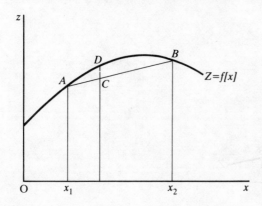

n-dimensional space. For example, if z is a function of two variables, $z = f[x, y]$, then $f[x, y]$ is said to be *concave* if

$$f[\lambda x_1 + (1 - \lambda)x_2, \lambda y_1 + (1 - \lambda)y_2] \geq \lambda f[x_1, y_1] + (1 - \lambda)f[x_2, y_2]$$
[A.2]

where (x_1, y_1) and (x_2, y_2) are any given points in the xy plane and λ is any constant between 0 and 1. The function is *strictly concave* if a strict inequality sign ($>$) holds in equation [A.2]. This implies that the shape of the function in three-dimensional space is concave or domelike when 'looking upwards' from the xy plane.

Quasi-concavity

This is a concept more directly relevant to the material in this book. Suppose $z = f[x, y]$ is *increasing in x and y*. Then, $z = f[x, y]$ is *quasi-concave* if equation [A.2] holds merely for any points (x_1, y_1) and (x_2, y_2) in the xy plane, which assign the same value to z. That is, any two points for which

$$f[x_1, y_1] = f[x_2, y_2] = z_0$$

Equation [A.2] can then be written as

$$f[\lambda x_1 + (1 - \lambda)x_2, \lambda y_1 + (1 - \lambda)y_2] \geq z_0$$
[A.3]

The function is *strictly quasi-concave* if the strict inequality ($>$) holds in equation [A.3].

The two-variable case is illustrated in Fig. A.2. The curve labelled Z_0 is an 'iso-z' curve – that is it traces out all combinations of x and y which give the same given value, z_0, to the function $f[x, y]$. Suppose A and B are points with coordinates (x_1, y_1) and (x_2, y_2) lying on the curve Z_0. Any point C on the line

A.2 Strict quasi-concavity

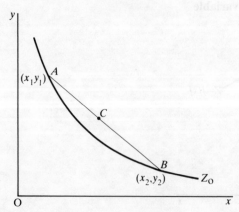

segment AB will have coordinates which are a weighted average of those of the points A and B, that is $[\lambda x_1 + (1 - \lambda)x_2, \lambda y_1 + (1 - \lambda)y_2]$. Equation [A.3] with the strict inequality sign holding therefore implies that the value of the z-function at the point C exceeds its value on the iso-z curve, Z_0.[1] That is, the iso-z curve must be *convex to the origin*. Notice that whereas strict concavity has implications for the shape of the function in three dimensions, strict quasi-concavity simply implies that the iso-z curves in the two-dimensional xy plane are convex to the origin.

Convex preferences

Suppose B_1 and B_2 are any two 'bundles' of goods. Then a consumer's preferences are said to be *strictly convex* if

$$\lambda B_1 + (1 - \lambda)B_2 > B_2 \quad \text{when} \quad B_1 \sim B_2 \quad 0 < \lambda < 1 \qquad \text{[A.4]}$$

That is, if the consumer is indifferent between B_1 and B_2 (i.e. $B_1 \sim B_2$) then he will prefer ($>$) any weighted average of B_1 and B_2 to either the bundle B_2 alone or the bundle B_1 alone. The two-good case is illustrated in Fig. A.3.

A weighted average of the two bundles B_1 and B_2 can be represented by a point such as A on the line segment joining B_1 and B_2. Consider the 'indifference curve', I, passing through all bundles of goods which the consumer ranks as 'equivalent' to B_1 and B_2 – that is the consumer is indifferent between all bundles on this curve. The curve must obviously pass through B_1 and B_2 but equation [A.4] implies that it must also pass between A and the origin[2] – that is A is preferred to any point such as B_3. Thus *strictly convex preferences imply indifference curves that are everywhere convex to the origin.*

A less restrictive assumption than strict convexity is convexity. A consumer's preferences are said to be *convex* if equation [A.4] is replaced by[3]

$$\lambda B_1 + (1 - \lambda)B_2 \geqslant B_2 \quad \text{when} \quad B_1 \sim B_2 \quad 0 < \lambda < 1 \qquad \text{[A.5]}$$

That is, the consumer is either indifferent between ($\sim$) a weighted average of

A.3 Strictly convex preferences

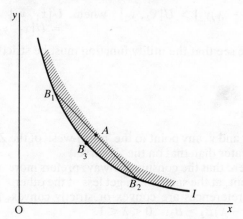

A.4 Non-strictly convex preferences

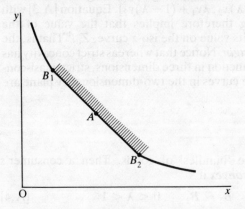

B_1 and B_2 and the bundle B_2 alone or prefers ($>$) the weighted average. The two-good case is illustrated in Fig. A.4.

The indifference curve passing through B_1 and B_2 now *either* passes between A and the origin *or passes through A*. That is, it passes to the left of the shaded area.

Notice that indifference curves that intersect the x or y axes (such as those in Fig. 2.2) and indifference curves that contain linear segments (such as those in Fig. 2.3) *imply that preferences are convex but not strictly convex*. The indifference curves have to be everywhere convex to the origin to imply strict convexity.

The reader will have no doubt noticed the similarity between Figs A.2 and A.3. In fact, it is not difficult to show that *if preferences are strictly convex then any utility function used to represent them must be strictly quasi-concave*.

Suppose the utility function is $U[x, y]$ and the bundles B_1 and B_2 consist of (x_1, y_1) and (x_2, y_2) respectively. Then

$$B_1 \sim B_2 \quad \text{implies} \quad U[x_1, y_1] = U[x_2, y_2] \tag{A.6}$$

A weighted average of B_1 and B_2 consists of $[\lambda x_1 + (1 - \lambda)x_2, \lambda y_1 + (1 - \lambda)y_2]$. Thus, from equation [A.6] strictly convex preferences imply

$$U[\lambda x_1 + (1 - \lambda)x_2, \lambda y_1 + (1 - \lambda)y_2] > U[x_2, y_2] \quad \text{when} \quad U[x_1, y_1] = U[x_2, y_2]$$

Hence using equation [A.3] we see that the utility function must be strictly quasi-concave.

Notes

1. Since $f[x, y]$ is increasing in x and y, any point to the 'north-west' of the Z_0 curve must have a z-value greater than that on the Z_0 curve.
2. We are implicitly assuming here that the consumer always prefers more of one good, provided he does not, at the same time, get less of the other.
3. If $B_1 > B_2$ then, whether preferences are convex or strictly convex, it should be clear that $\lambda B_1 + (1 - \lambda)B_2 > B_2, \quad 0 < \lambda \leqslant 1$.

Appendix B

Roy's identity and Shephard's lemma

In the n-good case the indirect utility function is

$$U^* = U^*(p_1, p_2, p_3, \ldots, p_n, m)$$

When the consumer has reached equilibrium, that is has allocated his total expenditure so as to maximise utility, $dU^* = 0$. Thus, totally differentiating the indirect utility function we have

$$\frac{\partial U^*}{\partial p_1} \, dp_1 + \frac{\partial U^*}{\partial p_2} \, dp_2 + \cdots + \frac{\partial U^*}{\partial p_n} \, dp_n = -\frac{\partial U^*}{\partial m} \, dm \qquad \text{[B.1]}$$

Totally differentiating the budget constraint and remembering that in equilibrium $dq_i = 0$ for all i, yields in the n-good case

$$q_1 \, dp_1 + q_2 \, dp_2 + \cdots + q_n \, dp_n = dm \qquad \text{[B.2]}$$

Comparing the coefficients of the dp_i and dm in equations [B.1] and [B.2] yields

$$\frac{\partial U^*/\partial p_1}{q_1} = \frac{\partial U^*/\partial p_2}{q_2} = \cdots = \frac{\partial U^*/\partial p_n}{q_n} = -\frac{\partial U^*}{\partial m}$$

or

$$q_i = -\frac{\partial U^*/\partial p_i}{\partial U^*/\partial m} \qquad \text{for } i = 1, 2, 3, \ldots, n \qquad \text{[B.3]}$$

Equation [B.3] is *Roy's identity*.

In the n-good case the consumer's cost function is

$$m^* = m^*(p_1, p_2, p_3, \ldots, p_n, U^*) \qquad \text{[B.4]}$$

Consider an arbitrary set of prices $\bar{p}_1, \bar{p}_2, \bar{p}_3, \ldots, \bar{p}_n$, a given utility level U^* and the corresponding optimal purchases $q_1^*, q_2^*, q_3^*, \ldots, q_n^*$. Define, for any other set of prices, $p_1, p_2, p_3, \ldots, p_n$, the function

$$Z(p_1, p_2, p_3, \ldots, p_n) = p_1 q_1^* + p_2 q_2^* + \cdots + p_n q_n^* \\ - m^*(p_1, p_2, p_3, \ldots, p_n, U^*) \qquad \text{[B.5]}$$

The first term on the right hand side of equation [B.5] is the cost of the purchases q_i^* at the prices p_i. The second term on the right-hand side is the minimum cost of obtaining the utility level, U^*, which is yielded by the purchases q_i^*. Since the q_i^* are not necessarily optimal for the prices p_i, it follows that $Z \geqslant 0$ and that Z will only take its minimum value $Z = 0$ when $p_i = \bar{p}_i$ for all i.

Differentiating Z with respect to each of the p_i in turn yields

$$\frac{\partial Z}{\partial p_i} = q_i^* - \frac{\partial m^*}{\partial p_i} \qquad i = 1, 2, 3, \ldots, n \tag{B.6}$$

Since Z takes its minimum value when $p_i = \bar{p}_i$, the partial derivatives [B.6] must be zero for these values of p_i. That is,

$$q_i^* = \frac{\partial m^*}{\partial \bar{p}_i} \qquad i = 1, 2, 3, \ldots, n \tag{B.7}$$

Since the original choice of the $\bar{p}_i$ was completely arbitrary, equation [B.7] holds for any set of prices. Equation [B.7] is *Shephard's lemma*.

References

Allen, R. G. D. and Bowley, A. L. (1935) *Family expenditure*. Staples Press.

Anderson, G. and Blundell, R. (1983) Testing restrictions in a flexible dynamic demand system: an application to consumers' expenditure in Canada. *Review of Economic Studies* **50**, 391–40.

Anderson, G. and Blundell, R. (1984) Consumer non-durables in the UK – a dynamic demand system. *Economic Journal*, **94** Supplement, 35–44.

Barten, A. P. (1966) *Therie en empirie van een volledig stelsel van vraagvergelijkingen*, Doctoral Dissertation, University of Rotterdam, Rotterdam.

Barten, A. P. (1969) Maximum likelihood estimation of a complete system of demand equations. *European Economic Review*, **1**, 7–73.

Barten, A. P. (1971) Preference and demand interactions between commodities, in: Hennipman P. (ed.) *Schaarste en welvaart*. Stenfert Kroese.

Bergson A. (1936) Real income, expenditure proportionality and Frisch's 'new methods of measuring marginal utility'. *Review of Economic Studies*, **4**, 33–52.

Blanciforti, L. and Green, R. (1983) An almost ideal demand system incorporating habit effects. *Review of Economics and Statistics*, **65**, 511–15.

Blundell, R. (1980) Estimating continuous consumer equivalence scales in an expenditure model with labour supply. *European Economic Review*, **14**, 145–57.

Bronsard, C. and Salvas-Bronsard, V. (1984) On price exogeneity in complete demand systems. *Journal of Econometrics*, **24**, 235–47.

Brown, J. A. C. and Deaton, A. (1972) Surveys in applied economics: models of consumer behaviour. *Economic Journal*, **82**, 1145–236.

Byron, R. P. (1970a) A simple method for estimating demand systems under separable utility assumptions. *Review of Economic Studies*, **37**, 261–74.

Byron, R. P. (1970b) The restricted Aitken estimation of sets of demand relations. *Econometrica*, **38**, 816–30.

Byron, R. P. (1984) On the flexibility of the Rotterdam model. *European Economic Review*, **24**, 273–84.

Chow, G. (1957) *Demand for Automobiles in the US: a study of consumer durables*. North Holland, Amsterdam.

Chow, G. (1960) Statistical demand functions for automobiles and their use for forecasting, in: A. C. Harberger (ed.) *The Demand for Durable Goods*. University of Chicago Press, Chicago.

Christensen, L. R., Jorgenson, D. W. and Lau, L. J. (1975) Transcendental logarithmic utility functions. *American Economic Review*, **65**, 367–83.

Davidson, J. E. H., Hendry, D. F., Srba, F. and Yeo, S. (1978) Econometric modelling of the aggregate time series relationship between consumers' expenditure and income in the UK. *Economic Journal*, **88**, 661–92.

Deaton, A. S. (1972) The estimation and testing of systems of demand equations: a note. *European Economic Review*, **3**, 399–411.

Deaton, A. S. (1974a) The analysis of consumer demand in the United Kingdom 1900–1970. *Econometrica*, **42**, 341–67.

Deaton, A. S. (1974b) A reconsideration of the empirical implications of additive preferences. *Economic Journal*, **84**, 338–48.

Deaton, A. S. (1975) *Models and Projections of Demand in Post-War Britain*. Chapman and Hall.

Deaton, A. S. and Muellbauer, J. (1980a) *Economics and Consumer Behaviour*. Cambridge University Press.

Deaton, A. S. and Muellbauer, J. (1980b) An almost ideal demand system. *American Economic Review*, **70**, 312–26.

Diewert, W. E. (1974) Intertemporal consumer theory and the demand for durables. *Econometrica*, **42**, 497–516.

Durbin, J. (1953) A note on regression when there is extraneous information on one of the coefficients. *Journal of the American Statistical Association*, **48**, 799–808.

Engel, E. (1857) Die produktions- und konsumptions verhältnisse des Königreichs Sächsen. *Zeitschrift des Statistischen Bureaus des Königlichen Sachsischen Ministerium des Innern* **8** and **9**.

Fisher, F. M. and Kaysen, C. (1962) *The Demand for Electricity in the United States*, North Holland, Amsterdam.

Fisher, M. R. (1958) A sector model – the poultry industry in the USA, *Econometrica*, **26**, 37–66.

Forsyth, F. G. (1960) The relationship between family size and family expenditure. *Journal of the Royal Statistical Society* (Series A), **123**, 367–97.

Fox, K. A. (1958) *Econometric Analysis for Public Policy*. Iowa State College Press, Ames.

Goldberger, A. S. and Gamaletsos, T. (1970) A cross country comparison of consumer expenditure patterns. *European Economic Review*, **1**, 357–400.

Gorman , W. M. (1959) Separable utility and aggregation. *Econometrica*, **27**, 469–81.

Hicks, J. R. (1956) *A Revision of Demand Theory*. Oxford University Press.

Houthakker, H. (1960) Additive preferences. *Econometrica*, **28**, 244–57.

Houthakker, H. and Taylor, L. D. (1970) *Consumer Demand in the United States 1929–1970* (2nd edn). Harvard University Press, Cambridge, Mass.

Jorgenson, D. W. (1963) Capital theory and investment behaviour. *American Economic Review*, **53**, 247–59.

Lluch, C., Powell, A. A. and Williams, R. A. (1977) *Patterns in Household Demand and Savings*. Oxford University Press.

Moore, H. L. (1914) *Economic Cycles: their law and cause*. Macmillan, New York.

Muellbauer, J. (1974) Household composition, Engel curves and welfare comparisons between households: a duality approach. *European Economic Review*, **5**, 103–22.

Muellbauer, J. (1975) Aggregation, income distribution and consumer demand. *Review of Economic Studies*, **62**, 525–43.

Muellbauer, J. (1976) Community preferences and the representative consumer. *Econometrica*, **44**, 979–99.

Muellbauer, J. (1980) The estimation of the Prais–Houthakker model of equivalence scales. *Econometrica*, **48**.

Nerlove, M. (1958) *Distributed Lags and Demand Analysis*. Agricultural Handbook 141, US Department of Agriculture, Washington.

Parks, R. W. (1969) Systems of demand equations: an empirical comparison of alternative functional forms. *Econometrica*, **37**, 629–50.

Phlips, L. (1972) A dynamic version of the linear expenditure model. *Review of Economics and Statistics*, **64**, 450–58.

Phlips, L. (1974) *Applied Consumption Analysis*. North Holland/Amsterdam Elsevier, Amsterdam.

Pollak, R. A. and Wales, T. J. (1969) Estimation of the linear expenditure system. *Econometrica* **37**, 611–28.

Pollak, R. A. and Wales, T. J. (1981) Demographic variables in demand analysis. *Econometrica*, **49**, 1533–51.

Prais, S. J. and Houthakker, H. (1955) *The Analysis of Family Budgets*. Cambridge University Press.

Smith, R. P. (1975) *Consumer Demand for Cars in the USA*. Cambridge University Press.

Stone, J. R. N. (1954a) *The Measurement of Consumer Expenditure and Behaviour in the UK 1920–38*, Vol. 1. Cambridge University Press.

Stone, J. R. N. (1954b) Linear expenditure systems and demand analysis – an application to the pattern of British demand. *Economic Journal*, **64**, 511–27.

Stone, J. R. N., Brown, J. A. C. and Rowe, D. A. (1964) Demand analysis and projections for Britain 1900–1970: a study in method, in: J. Sandee (ed.) *Europe's Future Consumption*, North Holland, Amsterdam.

Stone, J. R. N. and Rowe, D. A. (1957) The market demand for durable goods. *Econometrica*, **25**, 423–43.

Suits, D. B. (1955) An econometric analysis of the watermelon market. *Journal of Farm Economics*, **37**, 237–51.

Theil, H. (1965) The information approach to demand analysis. *Econometrica*, **33**, 67–87.

Theil, H. (1975) *Theory and Measurement of Consumer Demand*, part I, North Holland, Amsterdam.

Theil, H. (1976) *Theory and Measurement of Consumer Demand*, part II, North Holland, Amsterdam.

Westin, R. B. (1975) Empirical implications of infrequent purchase behaviour in a stock adjustment model. *American Economic Review*, **65**, 384–96.

Working, H. (1943) Statistical laws of family expenditure. *Journal of the American Statistical Association*, **38**, 43–56.

Yoshihara, K. (1969) Demand functions: an application to the Japanese expenditure pattern. *Econometrica*, **37**, 257–74.

Index

user cost, 26–7, 33 fn 10
utility function
   dynamic, 89
   indirect, 38–41, 79–84, 97
   quadratic, 89
   sub, 62, 66

vintage effects, 27–8

wage rates, 86–8
want-independence, 55, 58, 60–1, 76
   see also additivity

Young's theorem, 46, 76

Author index